Early Childhood CENTERS

D1370686

Written by
Margaret Allen, PhD

Editor: Stacey Faulkner
Illustrators: Darcy Tom and Patty Briles
Designer: Moonhee Pak
Production: Karen Nguyen
Art Director: Moonhee Pak
Project Director: Betsy Morris, PhD

Table of Contents

Dear Teacher,

We all want to do what is best for children—the children whose lives become a part of our lives forever—the students in our classroom. Each year that we teach, we struggle to use the time we are given with our little ones as effectively, efficiently, and meaningfully as possible.

As teachers, if we truly want to know what is best for orchestrating our students' learning, we need to watch them in natural play and during everyday interactions. What we discover is that they want to be actively involved in their learning. Sometimes they want to move during their investigations. Sometimes they want to play with others in a give-and-take relationship to solve problems and learn together. Sometimes they want to work alone, undisturbed as they manipulate objects, toys, and materials in their environment.

Sometimes children want help from us as they seek to construct meaning from their play-like experiences, and sometimes they want to do it all by themselves with no interference from anyone. Some children watch and observe carefully to learn, others listen to what's going on before participating, and others will jump right into an activity.

If we are to be successful in our attempts to meet all children's unique needs in responsive

ways, then we need to work to meet the early childhood standards in ways that are developmentally appropriate, academically appropriate, and learning-styles appropriate for the children in our classrooms. We need to provide multiple areas in the room with varying types of materials and activity levels geared to facilitate learning based on the various modalities of our students. **And with that, fellow teachers, we have just defined learning centers!**

I have three main goals for this book. The first is to provide information, or what we need **to know** about centers relating to child development and the standards. The second is to suggest generic materials, or what we need **to have** for effective centers. The third is to offer lots of ideas and specific activities **to do** during the center time experience. Use this resource to discover ways you can maximize your students' learning, minimize your preparation time, and, together with your students, build a joyous community of active learners in your classroom—all with the help of learning centers.

Dr. Maggie

Introduction

What is a center?

A center is a small area of the classroom where teachers have introduced a variety of hands-on materials and meaningful activities for children to actively use in risk-free ways. Its purpose is to help children develop new ideas, reinforce previously taught information, or meaningfully review concepts or facts. It is important to remember that centers do not always generate a product to "turn in."

What types of centers should I have?

Over the years, as programs for young children have come into and gone out of fashion, confusion has grown over the use of centers and the types of centers that should be introduced. The following three types of centers are appropriate for early childhood classrooms:

- **Developmental Centers**— traditional play time or exploration centers
- **Literacy Centers**—work time centers involving skills practice
- **Theme Centers**—developmental and literacy centers incorporating a common theme

Why should I use centers?

Learning centers are an integral and meaningful part of early childhood classrooms. Centers provide children the opportunities they need "to do" and "to practice doing" in order to internalize a process, master a skill, or understand a concept. In addition, centers provide teachers a manageable way to differentiate instruction so that children experience multiple ways "to get it."

Centers provide varying levels of opportunities for children to achieve the following:
- Explore, discover, and be creative
- Respond and record
- Engage in critical thinking and problem solving
- Develop social/emotional skills
- Use listening and speaking skills for different purposes
- Practice and apply content skills in meaningful ways

How do centers look?

A classroom with centers looks filled with active learning. It is a busy place. Children are using materials in various areas of the room. Some may be working with partners or in small groups. Others may be working alone.

The teacher is active during centers, helping to facilitate children's learning. She may be walking about observing, coaching, assessing with questions, or taking anecdotal records. She may be working with a small group, conferencing with an individual child, or (during kindergarten literacy centers) conducting small group reading sessions.

Planning for Centers

Every early childhood classroom is different. You will need to discover for yourself the optimum way to use the space and resources available to you. Use the following ideas to help you plan for room arrangements, materials storage, and working with limited space.

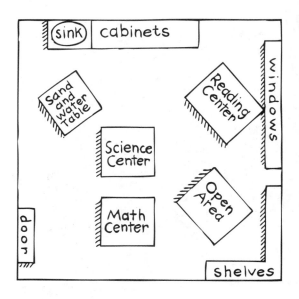

Setting Up the Room

Floor Plan Map

Sketch the shape of your room on a large piece of chart paper and mark all permanent features that cannot be changed. Use small sticky notes to represent moveable storage, furniture, cabinets, and center areas. Be aware of how the sink, windows, and doors will affect the natural traffic flow in your room. Remember to set aside a "quiet spot" for children who need a little space and to be sure that all parts of the room can be clearly seen. When you are pleased with how it looks on paper, try it. This provides a good starting point.

Give Us Space

As you think through your room set-up, remember to save space to create an open area for your circle time, class meetings, shared reading, dramatizations, and music and movement.

During center time, make this same open area available for children who are in centers that require more space. Allow children to migrate to the area, taking their center props, games, or activities with them.

Materials Storage Marvels

Self-Serve Cabinets, Carts, and Chests

Arrange center materials in cabinets, on shelves, in rolling carts, or in chests with drawers so children can easily remove the materials and work with them on the floor or at a table. Reserve the use of high shelves or tops of cabinets for teacher-used materials.

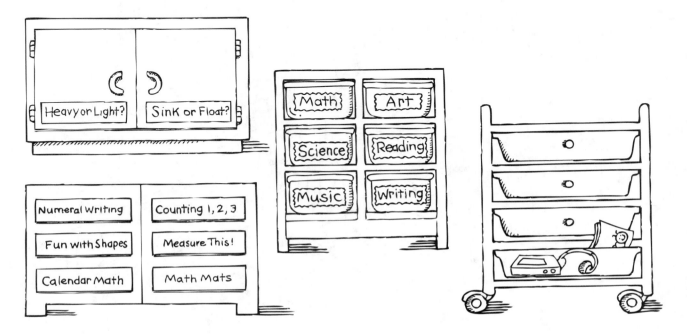

Color Codes and Labels

To help children know where to pick up and return center materials, create matching labels or use matching stickers to identify each material and the shelf, table, or cart on which it is stored. Or color code areas of the room and place color dots on all materials that go in that area. Take this idea one step further by creating materials maps as described on page 9.

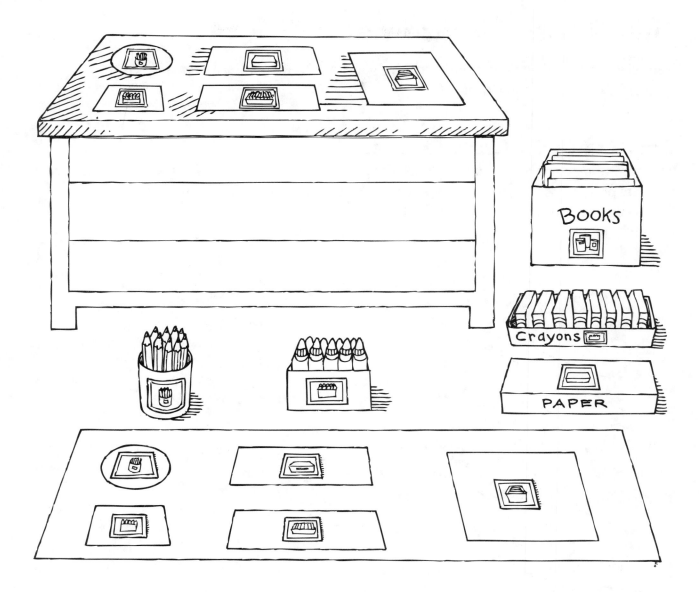

Materials Maps

Create materials maps using different-colored paper to line shelves, counters, tables, and drawers in a center. Position all containers for each area on the paper where they are to be stored, and trace around them. Use corresponding colored construction paper to create container labels to match the paper maps. When cleanup time begins, have children match container shapes and colors to the "footprints" outlined on each materials map to independently participate in the cleanup process.

As an alternative to color-coding, photograph each container with the materials in it and make duplicate prints. Glue one picture to the container and the other to the map for children to match. Or use a variety of other materials—such as department store or market ads, catalog pictures, or textured materials (such as Velcro, velvet, or sandpaper)—to match each container to the map.

Tiny Room Syndrome

Many classrooms have limited storage space. If you are exhibiting the symptoms of "tiny room syndrome," try the following ideas.

Cans, Crates, Folders, and Boxes

Collect cardboard copy-paper boxes, crates, cans, folders, large envelopes, and resealable plastic bags to create portable centers. Store them when not in use and bring them out during center time. Always keep safety in mind and never stack materials that are unsteady or too high, as they can be hazardous to young children.

Hoops, Trays, and Squares

Use hula hoops, upholstery fabric squares, carpet samples, TV trays, the back side of laminated posters, or straw beach mats to define areas where materials are to be placed and to avoid center materials mix-ups.

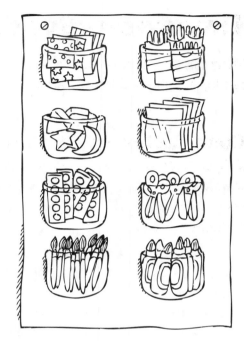

Shoe Pouches

Attach hanging shoe organizers that have clear plastic pouches to walls or the back of cabinets to store materials. These work especially well in the art, science, or writing centers. Children can see through the pouches and retrieve materials as needed.

Racks and Boxes

Use collapsible drying racks for big book display and storage. Use inexpensive, clear plastic shoe-box-size containers to store small books by theme, level, or subject area.

Center Dividers

Shower Curtains

Use fishing line to hang inexpensive see-through shower curtain sections from the ceiling as center dividers. These curtains give children a feeling of privacy while still allowing you to see through to know how children are engaged. Or hang a decorated shower curtain on the wall or drape it over a table to designate a theme area.

Match a solid-color shower curtain to a color-coded center area. Place it on the floor to define the allotted space for that center or to use as a "drop cloth" under messy play areas, such as the art center and the sand and water table. When cleanup time is over, sponge the curtain clean, fold it, and store it until the next center period.

Cardboard Display Boards

Create tagboard or cardboard displays to use as portable centers, portable word walls, or as center dividers. Or place them in front of stacked materials boxes or open shelving to hide "overflowing" materials and reduce sensory overload for easily stimulated youngsters. To enhance your display boards, sponge or spray paint them using calming colors such as light green or light blue.

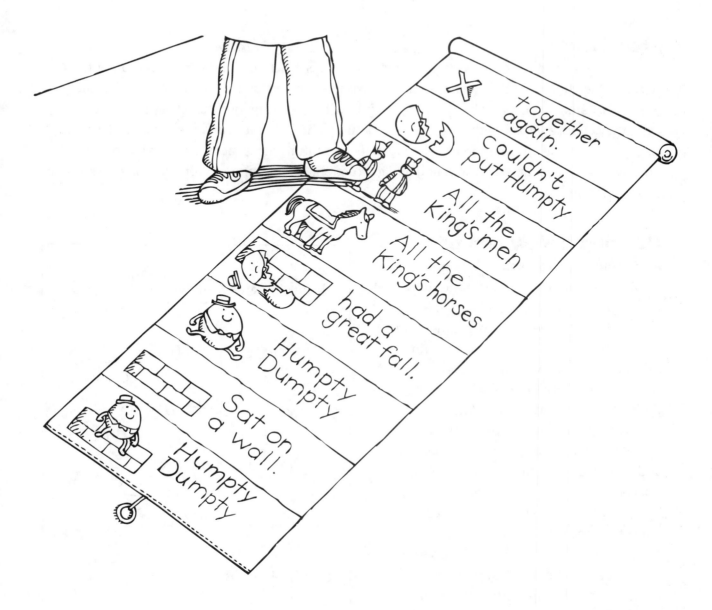

Window Shades

Use discontinued or inexpensive window shades as portable picture-noun, theme, or sight word walls or to provide step-by-step rebus and text directions for using a center. Mount the hardware low enough on a wall for children to use with ease. Have children pull the shades down to study the pictures and words or to read the center rebus directions; then roll them up when not in use. In addition, the shades can be taken out of the brackets and placed on the floor for "walk-on" stories and games and then rolled up and placed back in the bracket for group use.

Make additional shades highlighting other learning concepts, such as theme word and picture banks, math terms, community maps for social studies, and story walk maps. Store them all in plastic wrapping paper storage containers, which can be purchased affordably at end-of-the-season sales. Rotate the shades used to meet the needs of your class.

Getting Started

Start Slowly

Slowly introduce centers throughout the first few weeks of school. Start with developmental centers, since those need the least amount of explanation and/or "rule requirements" for safety purposes. Carefully observe the children to see how they are engaged, how they solve problems, what they choose to play with, their current maturity and skill levels, and their likes and dislikes. Use this invaluable information to help you plan your future center activities, small-group work time, and whole-group skills modeling and instruction. Refer to page 25 for additional information on assessments.

Opening a New Center

As you prepare to open a new center, display the materials on the floor to the whole group. Talk about the materials and ask for volunteers to show something they might do with the materials. During this process, work with the children to create safety and management rules for the materials at that center. Write down their rules along with a rebus drawing to aid nonreaders. After you have discussed and modeled using the materials safely, ask volunteers to help place each item in the appropriate center. This process is important because it allows children to see the transference of the materials from the discussion circle to the appropriate center. Post the class-made rules in the center. Then when conflicts arise, help children refer to rules that they helped create to resolve squabbles.

Our Center Rules

1. Be nice to others.
2. Walk, don't run.
3. Do your work.
4. Share with others.
5. Listen to others.

Adding Literacy Centers

After all developmental center areas are open and children have begun to work well during center time, it is time to introduce literacy centers. Explain to children that during these centers, they will focus on reading and writing activities, so they must be quiet enough to allow classmates to concentrate on their work. Make the contrast between developmental centers and literacy centers a "big deal."

Remember to introduce and model each center activity before putting it into a center area. Nothing (materials, process, or activity) should be new to children if they are expected to attempt working independently during literacy centers. How they complete the activity will be based on their own current level of understanding and skill development, but what they are to do, the processes, should be explained and/or demonstrated prior to the center period, even with open-ended activities used in early childhood. Always consider the needs of your class and children when choosing which literacy centers to introduce first. The following is a suggested progression. Begin with the Listening Post Center, then add the Reading Center, followed by the ABC and Word Work Center, and finally the Writing and Illustrating Center.

Managing Centers

Begin by having a few children at a time participate in the center until all the children have had the opportunity and understand the rules and options for activities. The key to well-run centers is model, model, model, and observe, observe, observe! Centers run smoothly when children know what materials are available, how to use materials in appropriate ways, and how to clean up when center time is over. Do not skimp on the time you devote to introducing centers, as it is critical.

The optimum management is self-management, in which children self-select their centers, complete the center activity, and clean up at the end of the center period. Over time, children will begin to be able to work in centers independently. However, this does not happen overnight. Use any of the following suggestions on pages 16–18 to create a system for center management.

Clothespin Cuties

Use poster board to create centers self-selection charts, one for developmental centers and another for literacy centers. Section off blocks of space on each chart for the centers you plan to use. Duplicate the center icons on pages 21–23 to label each section. Identify the number of children allowed in each center by placing the corresponding number of colored self-stick dots along the edge of the chart. Attach the poster board to a pocket chart.

Create Clothespin Cuties by gluing children's photographs to clothespins. Clip the clothespins along the bottom of the pocket chart. Have children find their own photos and attach them on the side of the chart in the appropriate block to indicate where they want to explore or work. If all of the dots in that center block are taken, children must select another center until their first choice becomes available. Remind children to move their "Cutie" when they leave one center and move to another. Set a time limit for centers to assist children in rotating to different activities.

Can of Worms

Duplicate the Can of Worms reproducible on page 19. Color and laminate the page, and cut out the can. Attach a magnetic strip to the back, and place the cutout in the middle of a magnetic board. On light green paper, duplicate enough copies of the worms on page 20 so that you have one worm per child. Write children's names on the worms, laminate them, cut them out, and place small magnetic strips on the backs. Place the cutout worms "in" and around the Can of Worms on the magnetic board.

Place a large, clean, center-labeled coffee can at each "open" center. To keep the cans steady, fill them two-thirds of the way with small rocks or pebbles. Add crushed green or brown tissue paper on top to represent grass or soil. To select a center, have children find their names on the Can of Worms board and attach them onto the coffee can at the center of their choice. Children must remember to move from one "can of worms" to another as they change centers.

Spin the Wheel —A Rotation Wheel for Kindergarten Literacy Centers
(Not recommended for preK)

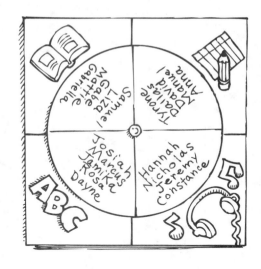

Divide a large piece of poster board into four sections. Label each section with one of the four literacy center areas. Cut a "wheel" out of poster board and divide it into four sections. Place children into four heterogeneous groups, and write their names in each section of the "wheel." Use a brass fastener to attach the "wheel" to the poster board. Invite children to check the board each day to see which center area they will work in during center time. As the wheel rotates, some names will be upside down, so be aware of children who need additional support finding their center. Or attach photographs of children's faces next to their names to aid them in identifying their centers.

Rotate the wheel each day for four days. Give children a special project on Friday, or allow them to visit the center area of their choice for Free Choice Friday. Change the groups every four to six weeks so that children have the opportunity to work with different classmates.

This management system also works well after you have begun small group/guided reading time. Call your homogeneous groups from the center areas. After your small group work is completed, have children return to their assigned center areas and resume their activities. Ask children to place any unfinished work in specified baskets at each center. Have children complete any unfinished work before participating in Free Choice Friday. Or allow children to take work home to finish during the week.

Center Signal Sticks

Duplicate the center Signal Sticks icons on pages 21–23. Cut them apart, color and laminate them, and affix them to paint paddles (paint stir sticks). Use the sticks to mark your centers. Place all center signal sticks into a decorated coffee can when not in use. You may prefer to have two cans, one for developmental centers and one for literacy centers.

Can of Worms

Worm Cutouts

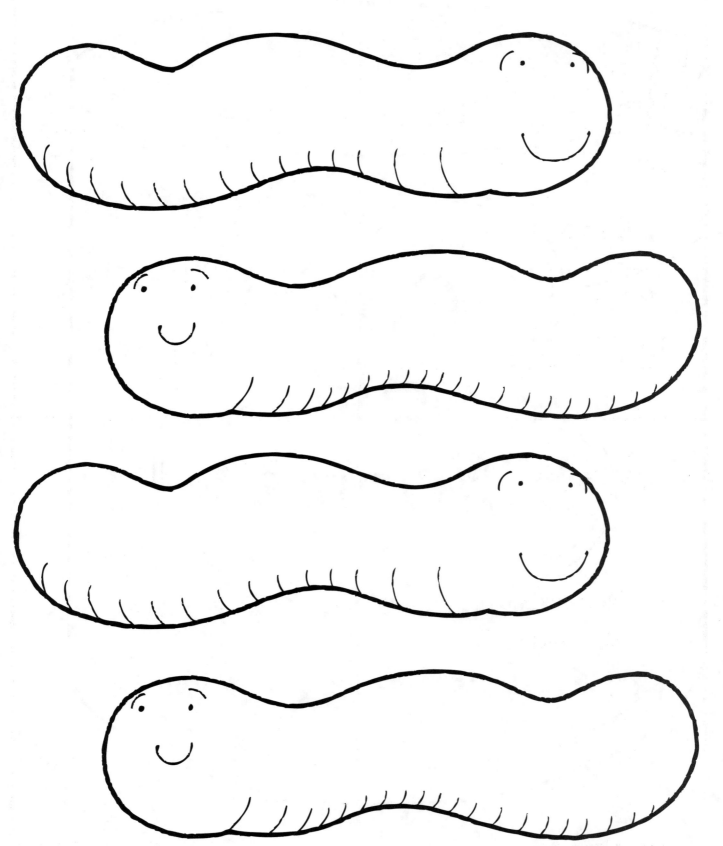

Signal Sticks

Math Center

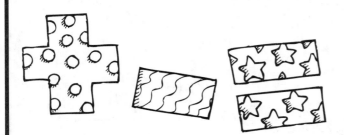

Science Center

Housekeeping/ Dramatic Play

Puppets

Signal Sticks

Block Center

Sand and Water Table

Art Center

Music Center

Signal Sticks

Listening Post

Reading Center

ABC and Word Work Center

Writing and Illustrating Center

Signal Sticks

Directions: Cut apart and color the two labels below. Tape them together to form one long strip and laminate. Cover a coffee can with construction paper. Attach the strip around the coffee can. Place center signal sticks inside the can.

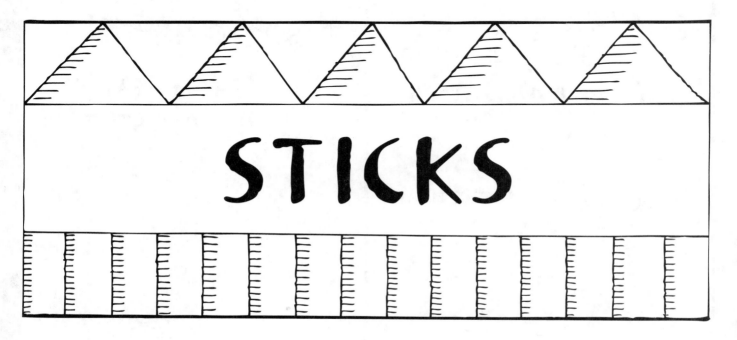

Early Childhood Centers © 2007 Creative Teaching Press

Assessment

Introduction

Assessment is an ongoing process throughout the year. Observations, interviews, checklists, rubrics, and tests are just a few of the numerous ways to evaluate children. Use assessments that are developmentally appropriate to guide your classroom instruction and to meet the needs of the children in your class. Knowing what information you wish to obtain and choosing a child-friendly way to gather it will help you determine the types of assessments to use. Three powerful assessment tools for teachers of young children include teacher observations, anecdotal records, and children's self-assessments.

Teacher Observations

Observe children in all center areas and over time. Be aware of what they choose to play with, how well they get along with others, and their strengths, interests, and current skill levels. Use the form on page 27 to make notes on the areas in which children may benefit from your intervention, modeling, and guidance, as well as information you may wish to communicate to parents.

Center Observations Date: _____

Student Name	Center	Observations/Notes

Assessment **27**

Anecdotal Records

Name _____		Date _____
Learning Behaviors	Social/Emotional Behaviors	Physical Behaviors

Anecdotal Records

Name _____		Date _____
Learning Behaviors	Social/Emotional Behaviors	Physical Behaviors

28 Assessment

Anecdotal Records

Anecdotal records are statements of exact, observable behaviors with no value-judgments. They are short written scripts of exactly what occurred or what was said. They provide a keen insight into children's unique learning styles and thought processes. Copy enough forms on page 28 for the entire class. At the beginning of each day, select a few children to observe and record. Attach their forms to a clipboard to carry with you during center time. Place completed forms in the children's individual folders, and prepare another group of forms for the next day. By the end of a week or 10-day period, you will have documentation on all of the children in your class.

Student Self-Assessment

Interviewing children to determine how they assess their own work and progress is invaluable. This form of assessment helps children compare their own work over time, set personal goals, and evaluate their personal growth. Asking children questions such as *What are you good at in this center?* or *What would you like to do better?* elicit incredibly honest responses and help you plan what to do next. Each week, give kindergarten children a copy of the My Center Time Record on page 29. Have children identify how they felt about their work each day at the end of center time. Collect and review the completed forms to keep track of which centers children participated in and how they felt about each one. These make great conferencing tools. Collected over time, they begin to reveal children's perceived strengths as well as their preferences, both of which are important to share with parents.

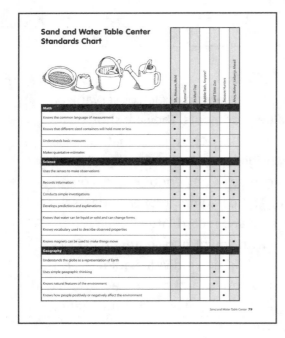

Standards

Early childhood standards are becoming increasingly common. Because standards terminology varies, we have adapted standards from McREL (Mid-continent Research for Education and Learning) for use in our standards charts. McREL has been a nationally recognized leader in standards-based education for more than a decade. Its preK–12 standards are a synthesis of standards documents from professional subject-area organizations and selected state standards. For more information on McREL, visit its Web site at www.mcrel.org.

Mid-continent Research for Education and Learning
4601 DTC Blvd., Suite 500
Denver, CO 80237
303-337-0990

Refer to the individual center standards charts throughout the book to see how the activities support student learning. Align the descriptions of the concepts, skills, and knowledge from the charts with your own state or district standards.

Center Observations   Date: _____

Student Name	Center	Observations/Notes

Anecdotal Records

Name _____ Date _____

Learning Behaviors	Social/Emotional Behaviors	Physical Behaviors

Anecdotal Records

Name _____ Date _____

Learning Behaviors	Social/Emotional Behaviors	Physical Behaviors

Early Childhood Centers © 2007 Creative Teaching Press

Name _____ Date _____

My Center Time Record

Directions: Draw a picture of how you felt about each center.

	M	T	W	TH	F
Listening Post					
Reading Center					
ABC/Word Work Center					
Writing and Illustrating Center					

Developmental Centers

Introduction

Developmental centers are the traditional early childhood centers often viewed as "play time." These centers tend to be open-ended and self-directed, and should be thought of as "play time with a purpose." Most developmental theorists believe that young children learn through their play as they "try on the roles of adulthood" and experiment and explore concepts in risk-free settings. Through these experiences, children build foundational knowledge for future academic content and develop the understanding necessary for working with other human beings, materials, and the environment.

Much is going on in well-orchestrated, teacher-facilitated developmental centers. Children are introduced to materials, concepts, and situations allowing them to meet learning and social/emotional challenges head on. Children are able to use their developmental strengths and preferred learning styles to support their experiences.

In recent years, much has been made of adding environmental print, functional print, and literacy- and numeracy-building materials to developmental centers, and rightly so. Explorations and interactions with these concepts are an integral part of the play environment and necessary for building a child's framework for future learning. Observing and assessing children in developmental centers provides insight as to children's development with oral language, fine motor skills, eye-hand coordination, numeracy and inquiry, and social/emotional skills.

The following four developmental center areas should be considered in prekindergarten, and all or part of them should also be considered in kindergarten:

Let's Explore! —**Math and Science Centers**

Let's Imagine! —**Housekeeping/Dramatic Play and Puppet Centers**

Let's Make, Mix & Measure! —**Block Center and Sand and Water Table Center**

Let's Create! —**Art and Music Centers**

123 Let's Explore! 🔍 at the MATH CENTER

TO KNOW

Young children are naturally interested in math. Innately curious, they seek to investigate and discover who is bigger, who can find the longest worm, who has the highest flying kite, and who can lift the heaviest stack of books. It is important to provide children with varied opportunities to explore mathematical concepts and develop problem-solving skills. As teachers, we need to acknowledge and foster children's natural mathematical abilities and their interest in number, shape, size, quantity, and pattern.

How Centers Help

It takes time for logic and reasoning to develop in young children. Centers enable you to provide children with a combination of child-oriented lessons and learning center experiences in open-ended exploration to help children develop as mathematical thinkers. Observe and encourage children's explorations with math materials and manipulatives, discuss their experiences, and ask questions to scaffold their learning and confirm their predictions and conclusions.

TO HAVE

- ✓ tubs, carts, baskets, trays, and boxes
- ✓ shells, buttons, plastic milk jug tops, keys, rocks, and foam peanuts
- ✓ linking cubes
- ✓ two-sided counters
- ✓ tongue depressors and craft sticks
- ✓ cards, dice, poker chips, and dominoes
- ✓ numeral and dot dice
- ✓ numeral spinners
- ✓ calendars, clocks, used watches, stopwatches, and timers
- ✓ play money; domestic and foreign coins
- ✓ masking tape, yarn, rulers, tape measures, yardsticks, and measuring cups and spoons
- ✓ walk-on number line
- ✓ flannel or magnetic board with shapes and objects
- ✓ balance and standard scales
- ✓ pattern blocks and attribute blocks
- ✓ geoboards with bands
- ✓ assortment of bag, box, and folder math games and puzzles
- ✓ number, color, and size charts
- ✓ dot stickers, stamps, and stamp pads
- ✓ paper of various sizes, colors, shapes, and textures
- ✓ assortment of markers, pens, pencils, and crayons
- ✓ numeral and number word flash cards

Math Center Standards Chart

	Move through the Month	Count "Flat Stanley" Style	Dough Numerals	Squishy Numbers	Ride the Wave	Shape Time	Ship Shape	Measure the Length	In the Jungle Roll & Count	In the Jungle Animal Addition	In the Jungle Animal Subtraction	In the Jungle Animal Patterning	In the Jungle Animal Graph	Count & Sing Math Books	Pattern Time
Numbers and Operations															
Understands numbers represent quantities		●			●				●	●	●			●	
Counts by ones to 10 or higher		●			●				●	●	●			●	
Counts objects		●			●				●	●	●			●	
Understands one-to-one correspondence	●	●			●				●	●	●			●	
Knows the written numerals 0–9			●	●					●	●	●			●	
Knows language for comparing (more, less)													●		
Knows the quantity of objects can change by adding or taking away										●	●				
Geometry and Spatial Sense															
Knows language for naming shapes				●		●	●								
Knows shapes can be combined to form other shapes						●	●								
Sorts and groups objects by attributes													●		
Measurement															
Measures objects with nonstandard tools								●							
Orders objects by attributes													●		
Patterning															
Understands simple patterns	●											●			●
Repeats and/or extends simple patterns	●											●			●
Displaying and Analyzing Data															
Knows that concrete and pictorial graphs represent information								●					●		

TO DO CENTER IDEAS AND ACTIVITIES

Move through the Month

★ Standards Check: Numbers and Operations • Patterning

On your calendar write the odd numerals in one color and the even numerals in a different color. Assign one movement to every odd numbered day and a different movement to every even numbered day. Begin the activity on the first day of the month, and let children count and move to the current day of the month. This provides great counting practice and helps get rid of the "wiggles" before beginning the morning meeting. Place the calendar at the math center for children to continue moving through the month.

Count "Flat Stanley" Style

★ Standards Check: Numbers and Operations

After reading aloud *Flat Stanley* by Jeff Brown, have children decorate copies of the reproducible on page 39 to look like themselves. String all of the "flat" children along a "clothesline" between two chairs using miniature clothespins. For safety, place the clothesline out of the way of the walking path. Let children count to rhythmic music playing softly in the center. Have children explore counting heads by ones, pairs of hands by twos, fingers by fives, and toes on the feet by tens. Children love this activity and will count and count and count!

Dough Numerals

★ Standards Check: Numbers and Operations

Use one of the recipes on page 130 to prepare dough for this activity. Have children roll balls of dough into "snakes." Place a 1–10 numerals chart in the center and ask children to form the numerals they see.

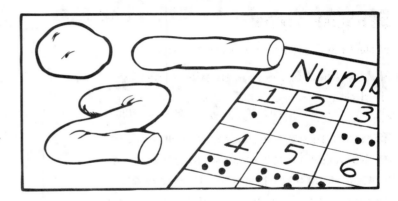

Squishy Numbers

★ Standards Check: Numbers and Operations • Geometry and Spatial Sense

Place finger paint into a freezer-quality resealable bag (just enough to coat the bag). Squeeze out excess paint and air bubbles. Lay the paint bag on a contrasting-colored sheet of construction paper. Have children try forming numerals using their fingertips. Place a set of numeral flash cards at the center as a reference tool. Remind children not to scratch the bag with their fingernails. Children will see the contrasting color appear in the indentation in the paint.

Variation: Encourage children to form squishy basic shapes. Or place colored sand on a cookie sheet, and have children draw a number or shape in it with their fingers.

Ride the Wave

★ Standards Check: Numbers and Operations

Have children sponge paint an inexpensive paper plate and let it dry. When the plate is dry, have them cut a wavy line through the center of the plate to create two pieces. Help children layer one end of the wave slightly over the other end, punch a hole through both pieces, and insert a brass fastener. Ask children to place linking cubes on both "wave sides" of the plate (enough to add up to a set of 10 or less). When children open the circular plate, part of the cubes

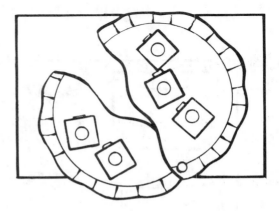

"ride the wave" and are removed from the whole. When children place cubes on each side of the opened plate and close it, two smaller sets "ride the waves" and are joined to form a larger set.

Shape Time

★ Standards Check: Geometry and Spatial Sense

Place shape stencils or premade shapes for children to trace, color, and/or cut out. Have children decorate the shapes to create an object from their home, classroom, or community environment. For example, a circle becomes a clock, a rectangle becomes a pet taxi, and a triangle becomes a clown's hat. Have children glue their objects to sheets of newsprint and draw background scenery to show their shape creations in their environment.

Ship Shape

★ Standards Check: Geometry and Spatial Sense

Place basic shapes made from tagboard or corrugated cardboard at the center. Ask each child to arrange the shapes on the table to create an object, such as a sailboat or a house. Have children place newsprint on top of their creations and place a teacher-made cardboard frame on the newsprint (old transparency frames work well for this) to hold the paper in place. Next, have children shade over the newsprint multiple times with the side of a broken, unwrapped jumbo crayon to create rubbings of their shape creations.

Measure the Length

★ Standards Check: Measurement • Displaying and Analyzing Data

Place a container of linking cubes, newsprint, crayons, and 5–6 classroom objects such as books, small dolls, and plastic spoons at the center. Have each child select an object and trace around it on newsprint. Ask children to connect linking cubes to determine how many cubes long their objects are. Have children count the cubes and write that number next to the outline on the paper. Ask children to return the cubes to the container for the next group of children to use. Taking the cubes apart from the chain is a good fine motor activity.

Use pages 40–41 for any of the math mat games and activities on pages 36–37. Prepare six math mats and the animal cards in advance. Copy the pages on card stock for durability. Color and laminate the pages, and cut out the animal cards. For variation use plastic animals for the manipulative pieces. Or create your own math mats and animal cards using a farm or backyard animal theme.

In the Jungle Roll & Count

★ Standards Check: Numbers and Operations

Place the *In the Jungle* math mats, animal cards, and a dot die in the center. Have children each take a math mat and place all animal manipulatives in a pool between the mats. Have children take turns rolling the die and identifying the number set of dots displayed. Have children count out that same number of animal cards and place them anywhere on their mats. The game continues until all manipulatives are used. Invite children to count all of their animal cards to determine who has the most, or have children see who had the least number of animals on their mat. Ask children to place all animal pieces back into the pool for another round.

In the Jungle Animal Addition and Subtraction

★ Standards Check: Numbers and Operations

Place the *In the Jungle* math mats, animal cards, and a dot die and numeral spinner in the center. Have children each take a math mat and place all animal manipulatives in a pool between the mats. Invite children to take turns rolling a die and placing that number of objects on one part of their mats. Then have children spin the spinner and place that number of objects on another part of their mats. Ask children to count both sets to add the total number of animals on their mats and then say their math problems aloud. For example, *"I have 5 animals in the tree. I have 2 animals on the ground. So I counted 7 altogether."* After their turns, have children place all animals back in the pool for the next round of the game.

Subtraction:

Place the *In the Jungle* math mats, animal cards, and a 1–5 numeral spinner in the center. Have children place 10 animal cards on their math mats. Invite children to take turns spinning, reading the numeral, counting out that many cards from their set of 10, and removing them from their mats to create subtraction problems. Ask children to present their subtraction problems aloud. For example, *"There are 10 animals in the jungle. I took 4 away. Now there are 6 left."*

Variation: For a higher-level activity, provide paper and markers. Have children write the addition or subtraction problems. For example, 5 + 2 = 7 or 10 - 6 = 4.

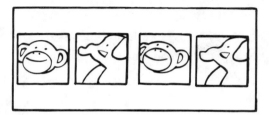

In the Jungle Animal Patterning

★ Standards Check: Patterning

Have children use the animal cards on their mats to create AB, AAB, ABB, or ABC patterns. Ask children to say their patterns aloud: "*I have monkey, elephant, monkey, elephant.*"

In the Jungle Animal Graph

★ Standards Check: Numbers and Operations • Measurement • Displaying and Analyzing Data

Choose three different animals and place varying numbers of each animal card in a container. Draw a large graph on tagboard. Have children categorize the animals by placing them on the graph as shown. Ask children to count how many animals are in each category and then "interpret their data" using math language such as *most, least, more than,* and *less than.*

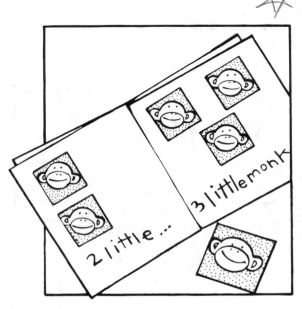

Count & Sing Math Books

★ Standards Check: Numbers and Operations

Cut colored copy paper and letter-size construction paper into fourths to create individual books with five sheets of colored copy paper and a construction paper cover. Duplicate animal squares, and have children cut them apart, count them, and glue them onto the pages of the book, ordering sets 1–10. Invite children to write the correct numeral on each page (with assistance if needed) to create a count and sing book to the tune of "Ten Little Indians." Example:
1 little, 2 little, 3 little monkeys,
4 little, 5 little, 6 little monkeys,
7 little, 8 little, 9 little monkeys,
10 monkeys in the jungle!

MATH LESSON

Pattern Time

★ Standards Check: Patterning

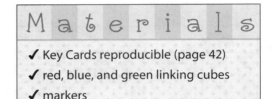

Materials

✔ Key Cards reproducible (page 42)
✔ red, blue, and green linking cubes
✔ markers

PROCEDURE

1. Have children construct a two-part (AB) pattern with linking cubes. For example, red, blue, red, blue. Let children assign a movement to each part of the pattern based on the Key Card choices. For example, if children decide that the red cube (A) equals "clap," use the hands clapping Key Card and color the cube on the card red. If they decide that the blue cube (B) equals a "high five," use the Key Card showing a hand up in a high-five position and color the cube on the card blue.

2. Have children use the linking cubes and the rebus Key Cards to experience the pattern by acting out the movements.

3. After children perform the pattern as is, encourage them to extend the pattern with the linking cubes until all cubes of the two colors are used. Invite children to perform the extended pattern using the colors on the cubes.

Variation: Later, create a higher-level center by having children create and perform additional patterns with the Key Card movement suggestions and the color linking cubes. For example, AAB (or red cube, red cube, blue cube) could be represented as clap, clap, high five. An ABB (or red cube, blue cube, blue cube) pattern would represent clap, high five, high five. An ABC (or red cube, blue cube, green cube) could represent clap, high five, finger flick.

Early Childhood Centers © 2007 Creative Teaching Press

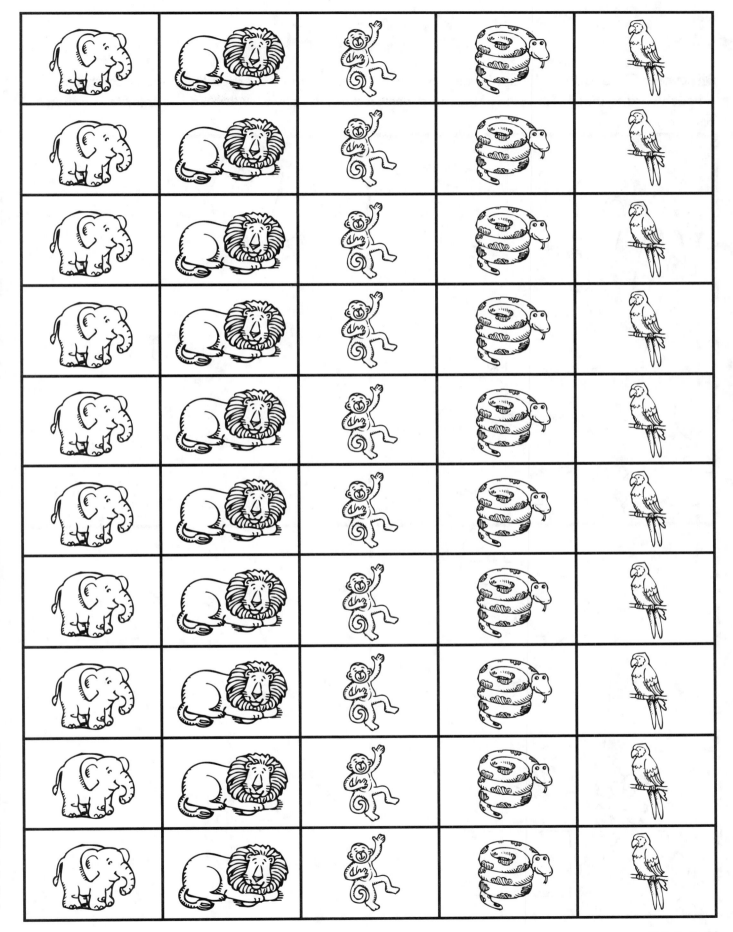

Key Cards

Directions: Cut apart and laminate the Key Cards. Use crayons or overhead markers to color the cube on each card to match the color of linking cubes used in the activity. Wipe off the color to use the cards again.

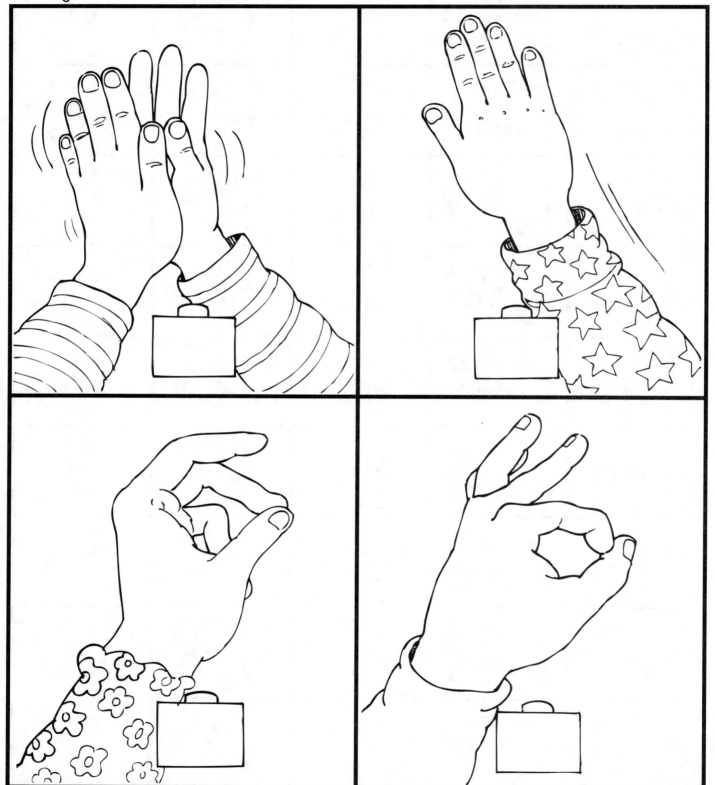

123 Let's Explore! at the SCIENCE CENTER

TO KNOW

Exploring science is an exciting and wondrous part of early childhood. Children seek to investigate and discover "how their world works." They question, they look, they listen, and they talk about their findings. Children investigate the passage of light through various materials; how insects crawl on the ground; and what sinks and floats, and why!

It is important to acknowledge and foster young children's natural abilities and curiosity as we develop their scientific thinking. Although young children may not understand complicated and abstract principles, they can wonder, explore, and discover ideas about plants, animals, and other objects in their environment. The following three major science categories should be included in early childhood classrooms: earth science, physical science, and life science.

How Centers Help

To carry out their scientific "wonderings," children need time to explore and discover scientific concepts in risk-free, play-like settings. It is through experiences involving interaction with people and materials, the physical and social environments, that children construct their own knowledge. Children are able to formulate and answer questions and use the "scientists' process" of observing, describing, classifying, predicting, testing, and reporting.

TO HAVE

- ✓ tubs, carts, baskets, trays, and boxes
- ✓ collections of seashells, rocks, feathers, keys, and marbles
- ✓ masking tape, yarn, rulers, tape measures, and yardsticks
- ✓ various scales
- ✓ assortment of bag, box, and folder science activities, games, and puzzles
- ✓ classification charts for animals, plants, and objects
- ✓ plastic cups, bowls, and containers in various sizes
- ✓ funnels in various sizes
- ✓ magnifiers
- ✓ eyedroppers
- ✓ thermometers
- ✓ stickers, stamps, and stamp pads
- ✓ paper of various sizes, colors, shapes, and textures
- ✓ markers, pens, pencils, and crayons

Science Center Standards Chart

	What Is the Weather?	What Is Mist?	Rock and Roll	Rock Etching	Will It Sink or Float?	A Balancing Act	Stuck on What?	Nature Is Grand!	Humpty's Hair	The Pocket Plant Wall	One Potato, Sweet Potato	Rocks—Hot or Not?	Squish to Mix Colors	Match Those Seeds and Plants
Scientific Inquiry and Communication														
Uses senses to make observations	•	•			•	•	•	•	•	•	•	•	•	•
Records information	•				•	•	•	•					•	•
Conducts simple investigations		•	•	•	•		•			•		•	•	•
Asks questions about observations	•	•	•	•	•	•	•	•	•	•	•	•	•	•
Develops predictions and explanations based on previous experiences					•	•	•						•	
Earth Science														
Knows vocabulary for different types of weather	•													
Knows weather conditions change	•													
Knows water can be liquid or solid and change forms		•												
Knows rocks come in many shapes, sizes, and compositions			•	•								•		
Physical Science														
Knows vocabulary to describe observable properties					•	•							•	•
Sorts objects based on observable properties														•
Knows objects are made up of different materials					•	•								
Knows objects can move in space (push, pull, sink)					•		•							
Knows magnets can make things move without being touched							•							
Life Science														
Knows living and nonliving objects are different								•						•
Knows living things grow and change								•	•	•	•			
Knows basic needs of plants and animals								•	•	•	•			
Knows plants and animals need certain resources for energy and growth								•	•	•	•			

TO DO CENTER IDEAS AND ACTIVITIES

What Is the Weather?

★ Standards Check: Scientific Inquiry and Communication • Earth Science

Place a variety of fiction and nonfiction books about weather in the science center. Ask children to explore and examine the illustrations of different weather types, such as rainy, sunny, foggy, windy, and snowy days. Provide a paper plate and arrow for each child. Have children illustrate different types of weather around the edge of their paper plates. With assistance from an adult, have children attach their arrow spinners to the wheels using brass fasteners. As children look through the books again, have them move the spinner to indicate the weather illustrated.

What Is Mist?

★ Standards Check: Scientific Inquiry and Communication • Earth Science

To help children understand properties of water and the concept that water has many forms, allow them to explore with misting bottles. Support children's background knowledge for this activity by exploring books about weather and observing pages depicting fog, or by observing a foggy day outside. Place a variety of spray bottles, plant misters, and empty perfume atomizers in the center. Ask children to observe what happens to the water in the air as they gently spray the air (not each other) with the water. You may choose to do this activity outside. Have children create their own mist and fog scenes using white crayons, blue paper, and gray paint thinned with water. To record their observations, have children use white crayons to draw the schoolyard on the blue paper. Then have children use large paintbrushes to paint the thin gray wash over the pictures. As the wash dries, children can watch the fog "creep in" as the picture begins to look foggy.

Rock and Roll

★ Standards Check: Scientific Inquiry and Communication • Earth Science

Supply your center with rocks collected on a schoolyard field trip, brought from home, or from a purchased rock collection. Add magnifying glasses, scales, and small bowls of water. Have children use magnifying glasses to examine the rocks to determine their color, presence of crystals, and any visible texture characteristics. Have children weigh the rocks to determine which are heavier. Help children develop vocabulary to describe the rocks, such as *jagged, smooth, rough, heavy,* and *light.* After the examination is complete, have children gently drop each rock into a small bowl of water and roll it around. Ask them to observe whether or not the rock's color or shine changed. Last, have children watch each rock to see if small air bubbles come out.

Note: As water seeps into more porous rocks the air trapped inside is released up to the surface as air bubbles.

Rock Etching

★ Standards Check: Scientific Inquiry and Communication • Earth Science

Place various types of rocks (from the collection in Rock and Roll) and coins in the center. To help children determine the hardness of rocks, have each child select a stone and try to scratch it with a fingernail and then with the edge of a coin. Ask children to think about which rocks could be etched, or carved, and which could not.

Will It Sink or Float?

★ Standards Check: Scientific Inquiry and Communication • Physical Science

Place in the center small containers of water and a collections basket of manipulatives such as rocks, keys, marbles, paper clips, crayons, pennies, twigs, plastic straws, and feathers. Have children play with the objects by dropping them in the water and watching what happens.

Variation: For a higher-level activity, use butcher paper to create a large Sink or Float observation chart. Have children create a "real" graph by placing the items on the "sink" or "float" side of the chart after testing them. Or for children who are ready, have them make predictions, test objects, and make individual paper copies of the Sink or Float observation chart to record their results by drawing pictures or using labels and words. Encourage children to share their predictions and results.

A Balancing Act

★ Standards Check: Scientific Inquiry and Communication • Physical Science

Place a balance scale and the same collections basket of materials from Will It Sink or Float? in the center. Have children test the weight of the center materials as they explore. Children may count out how many twigs it takes to balance a rock or how many feathers it takes to balance a plastic straw.

Variation: For a higher-level and more focused activity, ask children to count out sets of five of each of the objects and place each set on opposite sides of the balance scale. Ask them to determine which weighs more. Let children continue to explore freely with the objects and the balance scale. Provide time for them to talk to their center partners about their findings or draw pictures on a sheet in a learning log (page 54) to represent what happened.

Stuck on What?

★ Standards Check: Scientific Inquiry and Communication • Physical Science

Equip the center with a large tray of different magnets, such as a magnetic wand, a bar magnet, magnetic marbles, magnetic chips (from craft stores), and a large box of paper clips. Let children explore with the magnets and clips on the tray to see what they discover.

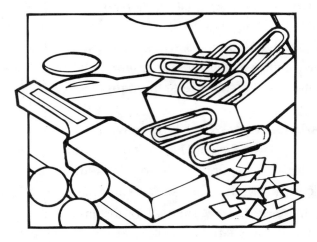

Variation #1: For a higher-level activity, and after children have explored with the materials, suggest that children select one magnet and predict how many paper clips, buttons, or magnetic marbles their magnet will attract. Then have children experiment to discover how many of the selected test items it attracts. Encourage children to choose a variety of magnets in the center and make predictions for each.

Variation #2: For a higher-level and more focused activity, add pencils, crayons, and learning logs (page 54) to the center. After children have explored, invite them to count and write or draw in their learning logs the number of paper clips, marbles, or magnetic chips that were attracted to their magnets. Encourage children to compare their results with a center partner. Facilitate children's thinking with questions such as *Which magnet attracted the most clips? Which magnets were strong and powerful? Which were weaker? What do the answers to these questions tell you?* Young children can be led to think scientifically over time. They naturally ask questions; we're "helping it along"!

Nature Is Grand!

★ Standards Check: Scientific Inquiry and Communication • Life Science

Place the following materials in the center: assorted live plants, cups, spoons, soil, "collection baskets" filled with dried grass, leaves, vines, bark, magnifying glasses, and books and charts of plants, seeds, and insects. Have children collect caterpillars and other insects and place them, along with small portions of their natural habitats and food, in small jars (with air holes) for daily study. After several days, have children release them. Or obtain a hermit crab to place in a terrarium with food and materials from its natural habitat. Allow children to visit it at the center over time to observe its characteristics. If the creature isn't doing well in the habitat, release it and find another creature to study.

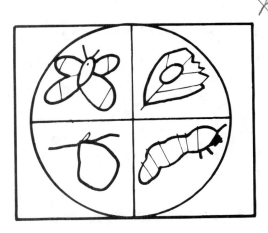

Variation: Obtain tadpole eggs or butterfly larvae and place them in a safe habitat. Allow children to observe the animal's life cycle over time. For a higher-level activity, let children record the parts of the life cycle they observed on the Life Circle reproducible (page 56). Ask children to draw what they saw, stage by stage, on their sheets. Have children place a Life Circle Cover (page 57) on top and connect the two sheets with a brass fastener. Have children turn their wheels to talk about the animal's life cycle.

Alternative Activity: Photograph each stage of the cycle. Enlarge the reproducibles to create a chart-size Life Circle and Life Circle Cover. Affix the photo for each stage to the circle, place the cover on top, and place in a center for children to manipulate and talk about as they move from section to section on the Life Circle.

Humpty's Hair

★ Standards Check: Scientific Inquiry and Communication • Life Science

Plant seeds in egg shell halves (cleaned and donated by parents). Store them in egg cartons on a sunny shelf in the center or under a "grow light." Birdseed is especially good for this type of planting. Have children draw faces on the shells ahead of time so that when the seeds sprout, it looks like the eggs are growing hair!

The Pocket Plant Wall

★ Standards Check: Scientific Inquiry and Communication • Life Science

Collect recycled clothing with pockets, such as old jeans. To limit raveling, cut off the pocket sections with pinking shears. Glue or stitch the various styles, sizes, and colors of pockets to a foam board or old tablecloth and display them in the center. Make sure the pockets are within children's reach. Have enough pockets for each child in the classroom to select one. Ask children to roll two different seeds in moistened paper towels and place them in sandwich-size resealable plastic bags. Have children place the bags in their selected pockets on the Pocket Plant Wall. Periodically have children check their seeds at the center, mist their rolled-up paper towels, reseal their bags, and replace them in the pockets. Continue this process until the seeds sprout. Then have children plant the seeds in soil.

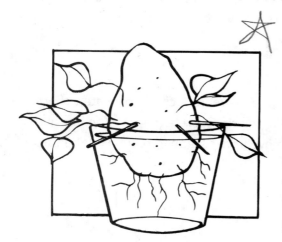

One Potato, Sweet Potato

★ Standards Check: Scientific Inquiry and Communication • Life Science

Place a sweet potato (with eyes) in a see-through container of water. Make sure you use toothpicks to hold the potato up so that only the bottom third is in the water. Have children observe the potato plant growing and add water when necessary. When the vine is growing well, place the potato near the window and watch the vine continue to grow.

EARTH SCIENCE LESSON

Rocks—Hot or Not?

★ Standards Check: Scientific Inquiry and Communication • Earth Science

PROCEDURE

1. Place the following materials in the center: rocks, ice in a resealable plastic bag, a blow-dryer, and pie pans or paper towels.

2. Have children, with adult assistance, set rocks in pie pans or on paper towels.

3. To help children see that rocks will absorb heat and cold quickly, have them first feel the rocks at room temperature.

4. Use the blow-dryer in 30-second intervals to heat the rocks. Have children touch the rocks to feel the difference in temperature. They will discover that the rocks will quickly become warm.

5. Take the warm rocks and set them under the small bag of ice for 30 seconds. Remove them and ask children to feel the difference in temperature. The rocks will have quickly cooled.

PHYSICAL SCIENCE LESSON

Squish to Mix Colors

★ Standards Check: Scientific Inquiry and Communication • Physical Science

PROCEDURE

1 Prepare one of the Make-It-Yourself Dough recipes in advance. Divide the dough into four equal portions. Leave one portion white, and add food coloring to the other three portions to make red, blue, and yellow dough.

2 Model for children how to place a marble-size ball of two colors of dough in a resealable plastic bag.

3 During center time, have children carefully knead the dough in the bag with their fingertips to mix the colors together and observe what happens.

4 Ask children to think about what happens when two colors mix.

5 Have children describe their findings to a center partner and then record their findings on the Squish to Mix Colors reproducible.

Variations:

1. After the initial experiments, invite children to vary the amounts of each dough color in other sandwich-size resealable plastic bags to repeat the activity and compare the resulting colors.

2. As a higher-level activity, add the white color to the primary color choices for children to mix and study. Help them discover that two primary colors mix to make a secondary color, but white mixed with a primary color creates a shade of the primary color. Children can create their own "Squish to Mix Colors" formulas to record in their learning logs (page 54), or they can add their new findings to the original Squish to Mix reproducible.

LIFE SCIENCE LESSON

Match Those Seeds and Plants!

★ Standards Check: Scientific Inquiry and Communication
Physical Science • Life Science

PROCEDURE

1. Gather seed packets for children to examine.

2. Place a mixture of seeds on a small tray.

3. Ask children to use plastic spoons to "scoop" seeds onto their paper plates.

4. Have children use an "open sort," or encourage them to sort by size, color, or shape.

5. Encourage children to carefully move the seeds away from each other using plastic knives and to use magnifying glasses to examine their seeds.

6. Provide time for children to talk about their sorts with their center partners.

Variation: Create a higher-level, more focused activity by having children try to match the sorted seeds with the fruit, vegetable, or flower packets from which they came. After their investigations, help children to discover that some seeds (corn and bean) are easy to match because they look like the part of the vegetable plants that we eat. Others (radish, melon, orange) are more difficult to match unless children have eaten the fruits and observed their seeds.

_____'s
Learning Log

Squish to Mix Colors

Directions: Color the first two circles to match the two colors of dough you mixed. Color the last circle to show what you discovered about mixing these colors.

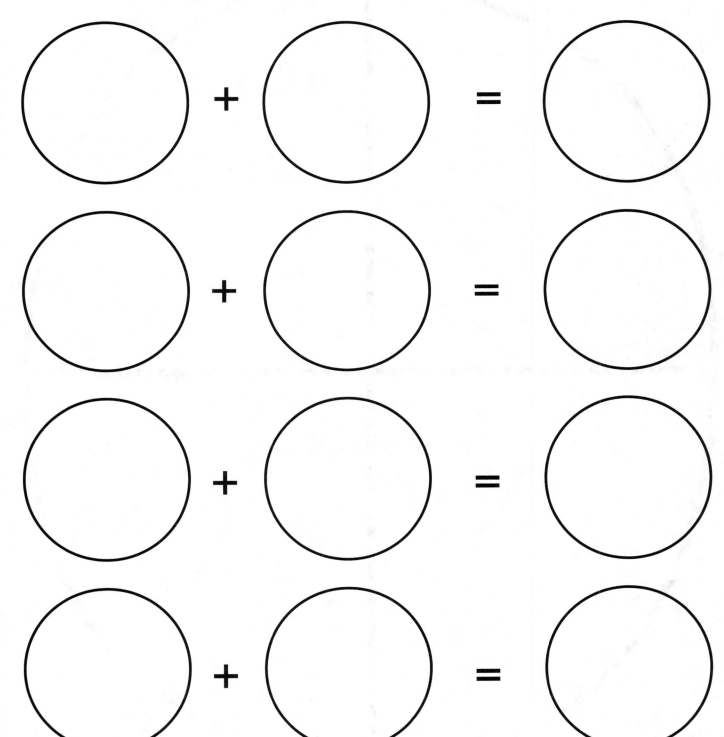

Early Childhood Centers © 2007 Creative Teaching Press

Life Circle

Directions: Draw each stage of the life cycle you observed. Cut out the circle.

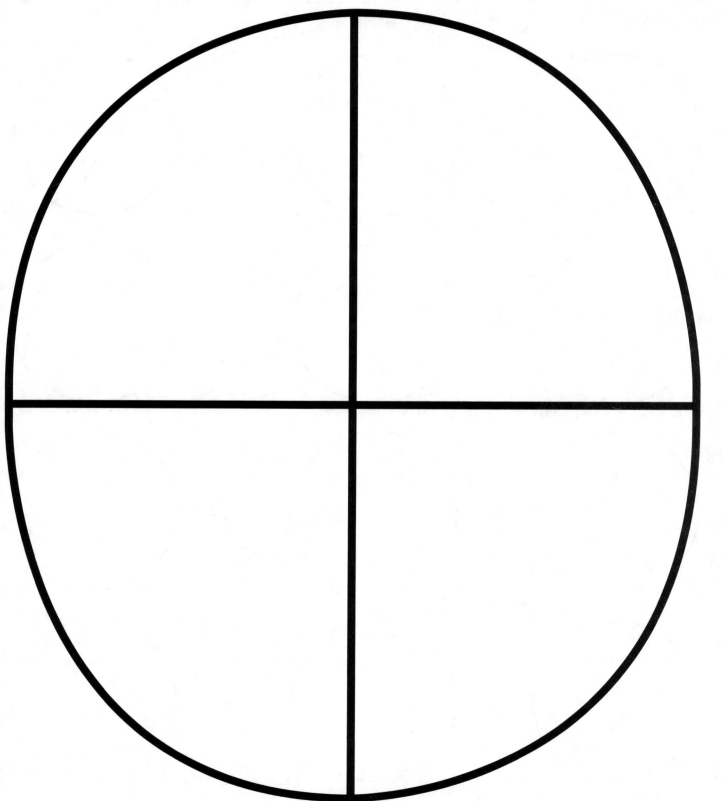

Life Circle Cover

Directions: Color the cover. Cut out the circle and the wedge. Use a brass fastener to attach the cover to the top of the Life Circle. Turn the cover to show one section at a time. Use your Life Circle to describe how your animal or plant grows.

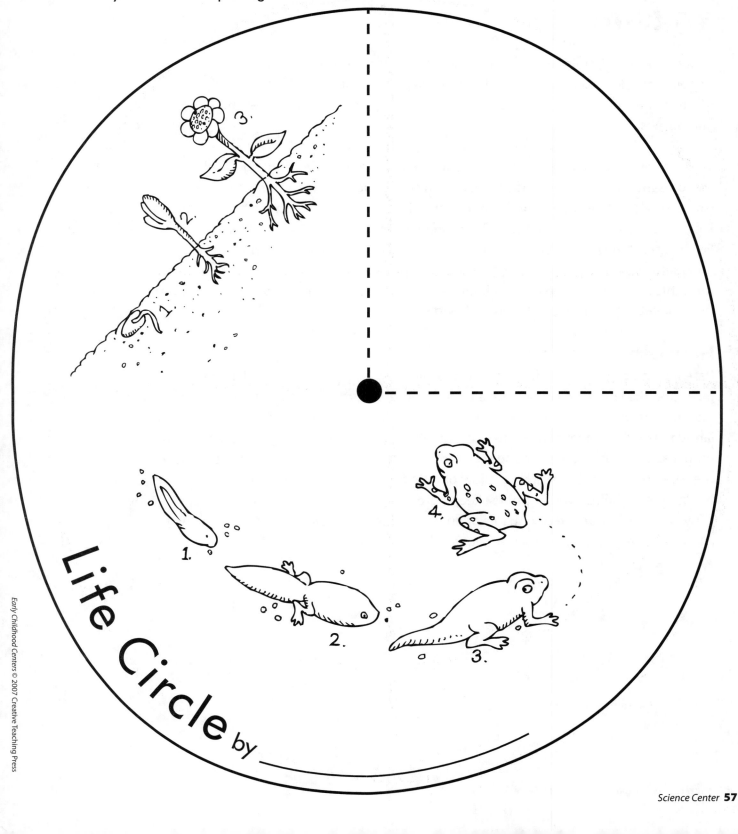

Life Circle by _____

Let's Imagine! at the **HOUSEKEEPING/ DRAMATIC PLAY AND PUPPET CENTERS**

TO KNOW

All over the world, children learn to speak and use language at similar ages and in similar ways. As eager preschoolers, three-year-olds begin to expand their two- and three-word phrases to create sentences. They grow adept at ordering their words to achieve their intended meaning and purpose.

Three- to five-year-olds use their accumulated knowledge of how language works to improvise and present their case. In doing so, they often create such magical utterances as "I goed to Grandma's" or "My foots are dirty." By age four, children are mastering most of the rules of language and are using more complex sentences. They enjoy talking and telling stories. Five-year-olds have an ever-expanding vocabulary, ready for use on command, and an adequate knowledge of word order and basic language structure. They can translate their thoughts into language to express themselves to fit each situation and every conceivable purpose—to ask, tell, request, demand, and share.

How Centers Help

Research indicates that the foundation for all literacy development is oral language, both receptive, the language children receive, and expressive, the language children use in everyday interactions. Experiences that develop creative thinking, problem-solving skills, and enhance language development contribute to children's cognitive development. Part of that development occurs as children create roles and scenarios during their play. As they act out their scenarios, they are building skills needed to follow plots in books that are read to them and in books they will later read themselves. The housekeeping/dramatic play and puppet center areas provide early childhood youngsters with lots of opportunities to play creatively, to interact with others, and to explore language as they act out roles both familiar and novel.

TO HAVE

Housekeeping Center Materials

✓ play kitchen furniture

✓ doll beds and multicultural dolls

✓ aprons

✓ kitchen towels, dust pan, small broom, mop and bucket, and paper towels

✓ pretend food and multicultural food packages and labels

✓ table and chairs

✓ plastic dishes, cups, glasses, silverware, and cooking utensils

✓ books and magazines

✓ lamp and rug

✓ rocking chair

✓ dress-up clothes

✓ radio, tape player, CD player, and audio tapes and CDs with multicultural music

✓ curtains over the window (made with paper and draped scarves or fabric)

Dramatic Play Materials

✓ housekeeping materials above

✓ "Magic Crates" materials suggested on pages 61–62

✓ blank labels

✓ illustrated word banks

✓ student journals

✓ markers, pencils, and crayons

Puppet Center Materials

✓ hand and finger puppets of animals, people, community helpers, and multicultural families

✓ tongue depressors, craft sticks, and paint stir sticks

✓ assortment of "wiggly eyeballs" in a variety of sizes

✓ stickers, cutout shapes, and stencils

✓ construction paper, scissors, glue sticks, glue, and Velcro pieces

✓ crayons and markers

✓ appliance box decorated as a puppet theater (if space allows)

✓ various pretend and/or real microphones or Karaoke machine

✓ cloth scraps, felt, and yarn

✓ paper lunch bags

Housekeeping/ Dramatic Play and Puppet Centers Standards Chart

	Dinnertime at Home	Let's Do Lunch!	To the Theatre	Let's Go to the Doctor	Off to Work	Let's Shop!	A-Camping We Will Go!	Puppets on a Stick	Spoon Puppets on Stage	Sock Puppets in a Bag	Soup's On	Eency Weency on the Way
Dramatic Arts												
Creates simple dramatizations								●	●	●	●	●
Engages in both fantasy and real-life dramatic play	●	●	●	●	●	●	●					
Creates props using available resources	●	●	●	●	●	●	●	●	●	●	●	●
Visualizes and arranges environment for dramatizations	●	●	●	●	●	●	●					
Visual Arts												
Experiments with a variety of colors, textures, and shapes								●	●	●	●	●
Creates 3D structures/arrangements using concrete objects/manipulatives								●	●	●	●	●
Uses a variety of basic art materials								●	●	●	●	●
Uses different media to communicate ideas								●	●	●	●	●
Economics												
Knows that a price is the amount of money paid for goods and services		●		●		●						
Understands basic concept of buying/selling		●		●		●						
Language Arts												
Uses writing and pictures to communicate information	●	●	●	●	●	●	●				●	●
Knows print and written symbols convey meaning	●	●	●	●	●	●	●					●

TO DO CENTER IDEAS AND ACTIVITIES

"Magic Crates"

Spice up the housekeeping center and enhance dramatic play with "Magic Crates." Try the following dramatic play scenarios using the suggested materials. Store the sets of materials in separate Magic Crates, and bring them out at any time. **As if by magic, children can become anyone they want to be!** Add labels to the items placed in the center, or create a portable illustrated word bank for children who want to write about their dramatic play experiences in their journals.

Dinnertime at Home

★ Standards Check: Dramatic Arts • Language Arts

Invite children to take on the roles of family members and pretend to cook, set the table, and dine to music and candlelight for a special dinner. Suggested materials include table and chairs, kitchen appliances, dishes, cups, glasses, flatware, tablecloth, napkins, cooking utensils, sealed, empty food boxes and packages (including multicultural foods), centerpiece for the table, radio tuned to favorite music, candlesticks, and candles.

Let's Do Lunch!

★ Standards Check: Dramatic Arts • Economics • Language Arts

Have children turn the housekeeping area into a favorite café complete with labels, menus, wait staff, patrons, chef, and cashier. Along with the materials in Dinnertime at Home, add a chef's hat, apron, pretend food, menus, play money, cash register, order forms for the waiters and waitresses, pencils, signs with the café's name, background music tapes, and a tape player.

To the Theater

★ Standards Check: Dramatic Arts • Language Arts

Invite children to become rock stars, actors or actresses, backstage staff, or ushers for the big night! Have children create plays, write play programs, make costumes, play music, and put on a show of their own creation. Suggested materials include chairs, dress-up clothing, shoes, boas, big hats and wigs (watch it during lice season!), large flashlight for a spotlight, pretend stage, microphones, music tapes and a tape player, tickets, and bowties for the usher outfits.

Let's Go to the Doctor

★ Standards Check: Dramatic Arts • Economics • Language Arts

Turn the housekeeping center into a medical office and
waiting room by rearranging furniture and adding
medical supplies such as a stethoscope, bandages,
white smocks, a flashlight, a scale, play money, pretend
credit cards and checks, an eye chart, RX pads, crutches, a play thermometer, stuffed animals or
dolls, tongue depressors, pretend "candy" pill bottles, a medical bag, a heating pad, and ice packs.
Invite children to take on the roles of doctors, nurses, and patients and dramatize a medical office or
veterinarian's office scenario during which they treat their sick dolls, stuffed animals, or classmates.
Children can weigh patients, write prescriptions, complete medical forms, and fill "prescriptions,"
examine each other for a temperature, headache, broken limb, or sore throat. Have books about the
human body, skeletons, and medical models available "for consultation."

Off to Work

★ Standards Check: Dramatic Arts • Language Arts

Invite children to pretend to work in an office and be business executives,
secretaries or administrative assistants, clerks, or accountants and have
"high power meetings." They can schedule appointments, write letters,
file papers, and give presentations. Have books about business careers
available in the center. Suggested materials include an office desk, chairs,
calculators, office supplies such as pens, staplers, paper clips, clip boards,
paper, a typewriter, an old laptop, envelopes, file folders, business cards,
a calendar, signs, telephone books, legal pads of paper, coffee cups and
coffee pot, easel, charts, and a pointer.

Let's Shop!

★ Standards Check: Dramatic Arts • Economics • Language Arts

Transform the housekeeping center into a store, and have children
become merchants and customers, write price tags, sell items
and make change, wrap gifts, run the store, and make purchases.
Have picture books about money, and department store ads and
coupons available for their use. Suggested materials include a
calculator with tape, receipt pads, pens, price tags, cash register
and play money, pretend credit cards and checks, items to be sold
(such as pencils, balloons, plastic animals, books, simple toys, and
play jewelry), shopping bags, gift wrap and tape, and signs.

A-Camping We Will Go!

★ Standards Check: Dramatic Arts • Language Arts

Drape a dark blanket or tablecloth over a table in the center. Clip-open a "tent flap" for children to crawl through to sit under their table with flashlights to "camp out" at school. Place any real or artificial plants available around the campsite. Provide children with a nearby stream made from blue bulletin board paper. Stock the "stream" with child-made construction paper fish that have self-adhesive magnetic strips attached. Give your campers fishing poles made from dowel rods, yarn, and paper clip "hooks." Children may choose to make a pretend campfire next to their tent, sing camp songs, or create pretend meals. Invite children to "fish" for their dinner.

When they return from their "campout," encourage children to write a letter to a family member about their camping experience. Be sure to create a portable Camping Words word bank with words and pictures for them to build their vocabularies and use to write or draw their stories.

Puppets on a Stick

★ Standards Check: Dramatic Arts • Visual Arts

Place numerous character cutouts such as a dog, dinosaur, gingerbread man, and bear in the puppet center. Provide children with glue, markers, wiggly eyes, rickrack, material scraps, and craft sticks. Have children decorate the cutouts, glue them to a stick, and voila—show time!

Spoon Puppets on Stage

★ Standards Check: Dramatic Arts • Visual Arts

Place a donated plastic wastebasket and a collection of wooden long-handled spoons and plastic spoons in the puppet center. Add wiggly eyes, glue, yarn scraps, pom-poms, material scraps, felt, and craft foam scraps. Have children decorate their spoons to create puppets. Then have children turn the wastebasket over and drape a colorful scarf over it to create a stage. Invite children to hide behind it or on the side of it and perform their puppet shows.

Sock Puppets in a Bag

★ Standards Check: Dramatic Arts • Visual Arts

For this activity, ask parents to collect and donate any stray socks, flat buttons, and brown paper lunch bags. Cut holes in the bottom of the lunch bags large enough for a child's hand to fit through. Place a varied assortment of socks at the center along with the paper lunch bags. Add flat buttons, glue, markers, yarn, felt scraps, craft foam scraps, rickrack, and pom-poms. Have children use the materials to make a sock puppet character and then create an individual "theater" by decorating their paper bags. Children place the puppets on their hands, and make them come up through the hole in the bottom of the lunch bag. Invite children to share their monologues with each other. Or have children work with a partner to create a "double theater" performance.

HOUSEKEEPING/ DRAMATIC PLAY LESSON

Soup's On

★ Standards Check: Dramatic Arts • Visual Arts • Language Arts

Materials

- ✔ Chef's Hat reproducible (page 67)
- ✔ Very Veggie Soup reproducible (page 68)
- ✔ plastic vegetables
- ✔ soup pot, ladle, plastic soup bowls and spoons
- ✔ measuring cups and spoons
- ✔ empty or pretend salt and pepper shakers
- ✔ clean, empty vegetable and tomato sauce cans (with labels)
- ✔ medium-size paper bakery bags
- ✔ scissors, glue, and stapler
- ✔ aprons

PROCEDURE

1. Duplicate the soup recipe, laminate it, and place it in the center.

2. Add to the center an assortment of plastic vegetables, a large soup pot, a ladle, plastic soup bowls and spoons, measuring cups and spoons, salt and pepper shakers, and labeled but empty vegetable and tomato sauce cans.

3. Have each child make a paper chef's hat from a paper bag and the reproducible. First, have children cut out the chef's hat pattern. Next, help children carefully turn the paper bag inside out and roll it up a bit to make a cuff on the outside. Then, assist children in sizing it by trying it on and scrunching it until it fits properly.

4. Glue or staple the chef's hat cutout to the cuff of the paper bag.

5. Have children don their aprons and chef's hats, "read" the rebus and text recipe, and use the center items to create the "Soup-of-the-Day" for their hungry patrons.

Variation: For a higher-level activity, have children create their own "soup du jour" recipes using large index "recipe" cards, drawing the ingredients, and writing as much text as they can. Invite children to "prepare" their recipes during the next center period.

PUPPET LESSON

Eency Weency on the Way

★ Standards Check: Dramatic Arts · Visual Arts · Language Arts

Materials

- ✓ The Eency Weency Spider reproducible (page 69)
- ✓ large and dessert-size thin paper plates
- ✓ stray socks
- ✓ markers
- ✓ fingerpaint
- ✓ sponges cut into small pieces and held with clothespins
- ✓ wiggly eyes
- ✓ pom-poms
- ✓ stapler
- ✓ glue

PROCEDURE

1 Make a transparency of the poem reproducible, and place it on the overhead projector. Read it to the children, and have them repeat it until memorized.

2 Model for the children how to create a spider puppet (see illustrated steps below) using two regular-size paper plates and an adult sock. Sponge-paint the plates whatever color you like and allow them to dry.

3 Cut off the cuff of the sock and cut it into eight strips to make eight legs.

4 Glue two pom-poms with wiggly eyes to the closed end of the sock for the head of the spider.

5 Insert the eight legs between the plates and staple them together. Leave room on two ends to slip your hand (with the sock puppet) in between the plates.

6 Have children create their own puppets at the puppet center using the same method as described in Steps 2–4, but with dessert-size plates and their own stray socks. Invite children to move their spiders as they recite the poem.

Variation: Use this same procedure to make any creature that crawls, such as "the grouchy ladybug" or "a little turtle that lived in a box."

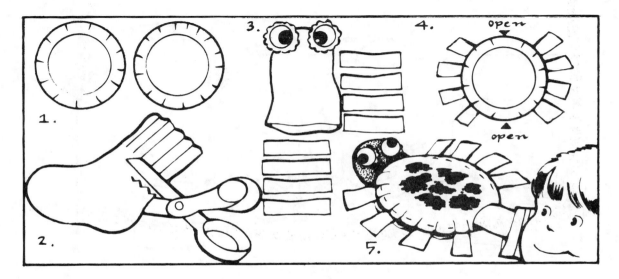

Chef's Hat

Very Veggie Soup

1 can of tomato sauce

1 can of corn

4 cups of water

1 potato

1 tomato

1 onion

1 teaspoon salt

1 teaspoon pepper

The Eency Weency Spider

The eency, weency spider

Went up the waterspout.

Down came the rain

And washed the spider out.

Out came the sun

And dried up all the rain.

And the eency, weency spider

Went up the spout again.

Let's Make, Mix & Measure! at the BLOCK CENTER

TO KNOW

The block center is a meaningful and valuable part of the early childhood experience. As children play with blocks, they develop spatial awareness skills. They use their imagination, develop creativity, and learn about number, size, shape, weight, form, and structural soundness. They interact with other children during their building projects and develop social skills.

How Centers Help

During center time children use language to reflect their feelings about their constructions and create scenarios around the structures they build. They use spatial sense as they use materials and fine motor skills to confidently create a product. They try on the roles of architect and craftsman. With project completion, children develop a sense of "a job well done," which increases their self-esteem.

TO HAVE

- ✓ block storage shelf or "block wagon"
- ✓ various shapes and sizes of unit blocks
- ✓ carpet or rug
- ✓ Bristle Blocks, Lincoln Logs, Legos, foam blocks, and dominoes
- ✓ cardboard boxes—closed and taped shut
- ✓ donated blueprints of a builder's model home floor plans
- ✓ toy street signs, traffic signs, and greenery
- ✓ toy vehicles such as cars, taxis, trucks, police cars, fire trucks, and airplanes
- ✓ flat wooden planks to create roadways and runways
- ✓ toy people, animals, and community helpers
- ✓ toy dinosaurs and zoo animals
- ✓ construction hats
- ✓ maps
- ✓ wooden barns and dollhouses with furniture
- ✓ ramps, toy cranes, bulldozers, cement trucks
- ✓ photographs and picture books of all types of buildings and structures

Block Center Standards Chart

	Checkpoint Weigh Station	Say Cheese!	Read and Build	My Home Town
Language Arts				
Knows writing and pictures communicate meaning	●	●	●	
Uses drawings to express ideas		●		
Knows print and written symbols convey meaning	●	●	●	
Math				
Knows process for measuring weight	●			●
Knows basic geometric language for naming shapes	●	●	●	●
Uses language to describe position and location	●	●	●	●
Knows shapes can be put together or taken apart to make new shapes	●	●	●	●
Understands shapes are useful for describing and representing real-world situations	●	●	●	●
Geography				
Understands maps can represent his or her surroundings				●
Uses simple geographic thinking				●
Knows common features in the local environment				●
Knows physical characteristics of local community				●

TO DO CENTER IDEAS AND ACTIVITIES

Checkpoint Weigh Station

★ Standards Check: Language Arts • Math

Add scales to the block center. Invite children to set up a checkpoint station with daily weight limit signs. After children "load up" their transport carriers with blocks, invite other children to weigh the loads and have the "drivers" remove excess weight before they continue on with their "haul."

Say Cheese!

★ Standards Check: Language Arts • Math

Young children often hate to tear down their architectural creations at the block center. Provide paper and markers for them to name their creations. Have children autograph their labels and pose in front of their structures. Take and print photographs of the children beside their structures. Place the photos in three-hole-punched transparency sleeves. Store transparency sleeves in a binder. Make the binder available at the center for children to review their previous creations with classmates or try to copy other children's creations. Add paper and markers for children who are ready to write about their work.

Read and Build

★ Standards Check: Language Arts • Math

Place construction theme books in the center. Include favorite picture books that prominently feature various structures, such as a hospital from *Curious George Goes to the Hospital*, a castle for Cinderella, a brick house for one of the little pigs, or the giant's house from *Jack and the Beanstalk*. Have children browse the books and then create coordinating structures. Photograph each structure, the "architect" who designed it, and the book that inspired it. Place those photographs in a photo album. Later, when this center idea is finished, place the photo album and books in the library center for children to review and appreciate.

BLOCK LESSON

My Hometown

★ Standards Check: Math • Geography

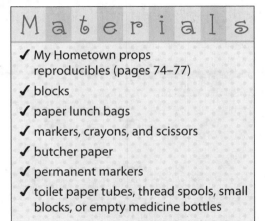

Materials

✓ My Hometown props reproducibles (pages 74–77)
✓ blocks
✓ paper lunch bags
✓ markers, crayons, and scissors
✓ butcher paper
✓ permanent markers
✓ toilet paper tubes, thread spools, small blocks, or empty medicine bottles

PROCEDURE

1 This center activity is a learning station created and used over time. Ahead of center time, and with the whole class, work with the children to lay out a town center with a surrounding residential community on a large sheet of butcher paper. Use a permanent marker to designate the streets and the town square. Draw boxes to show where the community buildings and residential houses will go.

2 Have children decorate the paper lunch bags to create houses. Ask children to decorate small boxes or wooden blocks to make the buildings.

3 Have children place their community buildings (fire station, police station, library, school, hospital, church, post office, and stores) around the town square.

4 Invite children to place their paper bag houses on the residential streets. Assist children in naming and labeling the streets and numbering their houses and buildings.

5 Have children color the scenery, people, and vehicles they choose for their town and glue the props to small boxes, toilet paper tubes, thread spools, or wood blocks to help them stand.

6 Ask children to navigate their way through the streets and tell how they will travel to get to landmarks, houses, and buildings. Facilitate the use of direction words to help children describe their travels. Ask questions such as *Can you find the hospital? Tell me how. Can you find 13 Honey Lane? Tell me how.*

My Hometown Props—Vehicles

Early Childhood Centers © 2007 Creative Teaching Press

My Hometown Props—Scenery

My Hometown Props—Family

My Hometown Props—Community Helpers

 at the **SAND AND WATER TABLE CENTER**

TO KNOW

As children explore in sand and water, they develop an appreciation of sensory play and materials. At the same time, they are developing cognitively, socially, and physically. Sensory explorations at the sand and water table also provide children with a sense of enjoyment and accomplishment, which builds their self-esteem.

Place the sand and water table on an uncarpeted or washable carpet area with plastic "dropcloths" covering the surface. Teach children to wash hands before and after use, to never rub any of the materials near their eyes, and to clean up their own spills before leaving the center. Some teachers find it helpful to have children bring old adult-size shirts from home, which they wear backwards as smocks with the sleeves rolled up or cut off. A broom and dustpan or a handheld vacuum nearby is also handy. Fill the sand table with rice for a different sensory experience.

How Centers Help

Cognitively, as children fill and sift, or pour and empty, they are developing math skills about size and volume, science skills using their five senses, and language skills as they talk about their explorations. They also use a range of skills to predict and test, quantify, and communicate their findings. Socially, they have repeated opportunities to observe others, share materials and ideas, and initiate investigations together. Physically, children manipulate the sensory materials and manipulatives added to the sand and water to develop fine motor skills.

TO HAVE

- ✓ water table or a large, shallow flat-bottom plastic container or small wading pool
- ✓ sand table or a large plastic or wooden container
- ✓ play sand and rice
- ✓ sand toys, molds, measuring utensils, funnels, sifters, and buckets
- ✓ water toys, animals, seashells, and boats
- ✓ measuring cups, spoons, scoops, and ladles

- ✓ picture books with ocean, fish, seashore, or desert topics
- ✓ plastic containers, clear tubing, and squirt bottles
- ✓ small fishnets
- ✓ large plastic drop cloth, vinyl tablecloth or shower curtain, and sponges
- ✓ small broom, dustpan, towels, and handheld vacuum cleaner

Sand and Water Table Center Standards Chart

	Sift, Measure, Mold	Funnel Time	It's Mud Day	Bubble Bath, Anyone?	Sand Table Zoo	Treasure Hunters	Ahoy, Matey! Icebergs Ahead!
Math							
Knows the common language of measurement	●						
Knows that different-sized containers will hold more or less	●						
Understands basic measures	●	●	●		●		
Makes quantative estimates	●		●		●		
Science							
Uses the senses to make observations	●	●	●	●	●	●	●
Records information						●	●
Conducts simple investigations	●	●	●	●	●	●	●
Develops predictions and explanations		●	●	●	●		
Knows that water can be liquid or solid and can change forms						●	
Knows vocabulary used to describe observed properties		●				●	
Knows magnets can be used to make things move							●
Geography							
Understands the globe as a representation of Earth						●	
Uses simple geographic thinking					●	●	
Knows natural features of the environment					●		
Knows how people positively or negatively affect the environment						●	

TO DO CENTER IDEAS AND ACTIVITIES

Sift, Measure, Mold

★ Standards Check: Math • Science

Add molds, sifters, measuring utensils, and buckets to the sand table. Provide spray bottles of water. Have children predict how much sand they need to fill a mold. Then have them measure the amount of sand they believe they need, sift it into the mold, spray with water to hold the mold together, and turn it over to place the mold upon the sand in the table.

Funnel Time

★ Standards Check: Math • Science

Add various-size funnels and containers to the water or sand table to encourage children to measure and pour without spilling as they move sand or water from one container to another. When using the water table, add a scented oil such as lavender, peppermint, spearmint, or rose hips for some "smelly" fun. As children measure, pour, and funnel water, they do so fragrantly!

It's Mud Day

★ Standards Check: Math • Science

Place extra-large resealable plastic bags, potting soil, a container of water, and measuring cups in the center. Let each small group measure three cups of soil and one cup of water to place in the bag. Help children press out all of the air from the plastic bag and then close and seal it. Let children "play in the mud" the clean way by mixing the dirt and water inside the bag to make mud.

Bubble Bath, Anyone?

★ Standards Check: Math • Science

Place large plastic bowls filled with warm water in the center. Add liquid dish soap to the water. Provide children with a variety of bubble blowers, straws, a whisk, and a handheld eggbeater to generate and blow bubbles. After the bubble exploration, let children add plastic animals or dolls to the center to provide them with a nice, relaxing bubble bath! Prior to this center activity, or directly after it, read *The Bubble Factory* by Tomie de Paola.

Sand Table Zoo

★ Standards Check: Math • Science • Geography

Add strawberry crates, zoo animals, and plastic scenery such as plastic rocks, bushes, and trees to the sand table. Have children dig in and excavate sand to create mountains, ponds (fill with crushed blue paper), shaded areas, and various zoo animal display areas. Have children turn strawberry crates upside down to contain any animals they don't want to get away.

SAND TABLE LESSON

Treasure Hunters

★ Standards Check: Science

PROCEDURE

1. Bury small plastic and magnetic items in the sand at various depths.

2. Have children "hunt" for treasure by sifting cups, bowls, or spoonfuls of sand. If a treasure is found, they "salvage" it with their magnets.

3. Label two buckets *Treasure* and *Other* to hold the day's "take."

4. Have children drop their magnetic discoveries into the bucket labeled *Treasure* and their nonmagnetic discoveries into the bucket labeled *Other*.

5. Have children use magnifying glasses to examine all "treasures" and pretend to determine each treasure's worth.

Variation: For a higher-level activity, add markers and learning logs to the center. Have children draw pictures and make labels to create "treasure reports" to turn into the newspaper. Invite some children to pretend to be newscasters and camera operators, and allow them to interview the treasure hunters for a television news spot.

Materials

- ✔ learning log reproducible (page 54)
- ✔ sand table
- ✔ bar magnets
- ✔ magnetic items, such as various styles and shapes of refrigerator magnets, toy coins with adhesive magnetic strips glued to the backs, and small metal toys
- ✔ small plastic toys
- ✔ measuring cups, spoons, and bowls
- ✔ sifters
- ✔ two plastic sand buckets
- ✔ magnifying glasses
- ✔ pretend news video camera
- ✔ play microphone

WATER TABLE LESSON

Ahoy, Matey! Icebergs Ahead!

★ Standards Check: Science • Geography

Materials

- ✓ learning log reproducible (page 54)
- ✓ plastic containers of frozen water (with debris if desired)
- ✓ map of the U.S. showing Alaska
- ✓ globe
- ✓ water table
- ✓ thermometer
- ✓ toy ships and toy Arctic tundra land and water animals
- ✓ strainers and small fishnets

PROCEDURE

1. Fill various containers with water and freeze them overnight. Add debris such as shells, twigs, pebbles, and leaves to some of the containers before freezing.

2. Display a globe and a map of Alaska in the center. Help children identify Alaska on the map and on the globe.

3. Have children use a thermometer to measure the temperature of the water in the water table.

4. Add the "icebergs" to the water table along with toy ships to float in the "Alaskan" waters. Add sea animals native to the frigid environment and to the Alaskan region of the United States for children to play with.

5. As the icebergs melt, debris will be left in the water. Have children act as environmentalists and decide what to do. Ask questions such as *Does the debris stay or will you remove it using strainers and nets?*

6. After the icebergs have melted, have children check the water temperature again with the thermometer and discuss any changes.

Variation: For children who are ready, have them record the temperatures in their learning logs by drawing side-by-side pictures of the water without ice and with ice and labeling the pictures with the temperatures.

Let's Create! ♪ at the ART CENTER

TO KNOW

One of the greatest drives human beings have is to express themselves. Young children are no exception. As children learn about line, shape, design, color, texture, and size, they not only experiment with concepts modeled during whole group lessons but also express their own creative ideas.

Children's artistic investigations are often based on physical explorations, such as manipulating clay, finger painting, or working with collage materials, which develop fine motor skills. In addition, early childhood is a time when children are developing their own imagination and multiple ways of looking at objects, materials, and media. Integrating art in all areas of the curriculum helps to strengthen children's understanding of the concepts they are learning.

Art and Math—Art develops math concepts as children explore depth, proportion, shape, and size.

Art and Science—Art develops science knowledge as children study line, number of extremities of animals, and color exploration, such as separation of light into the colors of the rainbow.

Art and Language Arts—When art is connected to language arts, children develop vocabularies filled with interesting descriptive words and the ability to make comparisons between their artistic creations and nature. Children use language to describe the appearance of famous artists' art prints and how the art makes them feel.

Art and Music—When art and music are connected, children benefit doubly as both media encourage children's ability toward self-expression and originality.

How Centers Help

The art center provides children time for free exploration and creative play with various media. The art center also provides opportunities for children to make inter-curricular connections and develop their ability to critique and appreciate fine art. The art center is a fun place to work independently or in cooperation with others to develop and strengthen concepts and skills.

TO HAVE

- ✓ finger paint and tempera paint
- ✓ watercolors and watercolor pencils
- ✓ brushes of various sizes
- ✓ clay and homemade dough
- ✓ sponges of various shapes and sizes
- ✓ various types of paper including fingerpaint paper
- ✓ stamps and stamp pads
- ✓ wallpaper samples
- ✓ fabric swatches and remnants
- ✓ scissors
- ✓ pencils, pens, markers, colored pencils, crayons, and chalk
- ✓ tape, glue sticks, and glue bottles
- ✓ collage materials
- ✓ art prints
- ✓ art books about artists' lives and work
- ✓ newspapers and magazines
- ✓ yarn, ribbon, string, and straws
- ✓ various colors of craft sticks and tongue depressors

Art Center Standards Chart

Visual Arts	Rainbows of Our Own	Art—Classical Style	Sponge-It	"Give Me Five" Prints	Yarn, Ribbon, and String Painting	Cow-Chalk Scenes—Moo! Moo!	Happy/Sad Watercolor Scenes
Experiments with various colors, textures, and shapes	●	●	●	●	●	●	●
Creates 3D structures/arrangements using concrete materials/manipulatives	●	●	●	●	●	●	●
Uses variety of basic art materials	●	●	●	●	●	●	●
Knows names of basic colors	●	●	●	●	●	●	●
Uses art to communicate ideas		●				●	●

TO DO CENTER IDEAS AND ACTIVITIES

Rainbows of Our Own

★ Standards Check: Visual Arts

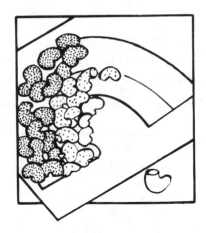

Dye small elbow macaroni the colors of the rainbow by placing 3–5 drops of food coloring and 2 tablespoons of rubbing alcohol in a resealable plastic bag. Add the macaroni, seal the bag, and shake it until the color appears evenly distributed. Spread the macaroni on paper towels to dry. Invite children to squirt glue in a large arc on construction paper and glue one color of macaroni at a time. Have them continue to add smaller and smaller arcs of glue and the remaining colors of macaroni until the rainbow is complete.

Art—Classical Style

★ Standards Check: Visual Arts

Have children paint to music using watercolors or tempera paint. Experiment with many different kinds of music and papers of different sizes. Watch in amazement at the variety of pictures that will be created. Some children prefer the easel, while others prefer to sit and work at a table with a smaller sheet of paper. Children's classics such as *Peter and the Wolf* and the *Peer Gynt Suites* are excellent for this center activity. Have children listen to a low volume CD placed in the center or use individual cassette players with headphones.

Sponge-It

★ Standards Check: Visual Arts

Cut inexpensive sponges into cubes. Scrunch the bottom part of the sponge and squeeze it into a clothespin to create a Sponge-It paintbrush. Provide a variety of paper and various colors of finger paint for children to sponge paint designs or pictures.

Variation: Use shape, numeral, or letter sponges for children to sponge paint with. Cut a slit in the back of each sponge, insert a craft stick to create a holder, and glue it into position. After the glue has dried, have children use the various sponges to create collage scenes or spell words or names to label their work.

"Give Me Five" Prints

★ Standards Check: Visual Arts

Place several paper towels in a foam tray. Pour washable paint onto the paper towels, and give it time to soak in to create a paint stamp pad. Place a variety of paper sizes in the center. Have children press each hand onto the stamp pad and use their "hand stampers" to print onto paper. After children wash their hands, have them autograph their prints and display them.

Yarn, Ribbon, and String Painting

★ Standards Check: Visual Arts

Place 9- to 11-inch lengths of yarn, narrow ribbon, and string in the center along with white construction paper. Prefold the paper vertically and crease well. With the sheet open, have children select one of the lengths of yarn, ribbon, or string, dip ¾ of it into a tray of paint, and arrange the painted string on the right half of the paper, leaving a "tail" hanging off at the bottom. Show children how to carefully fold the left half of the paper over the string and press firmly. Next, have children pull out the string by the "tail" and open the paper to examine the print left behind. When the paint dries, children can shade the background with crayons, draw pictures around the string imprint, or glue cutout pictures to create a scene.

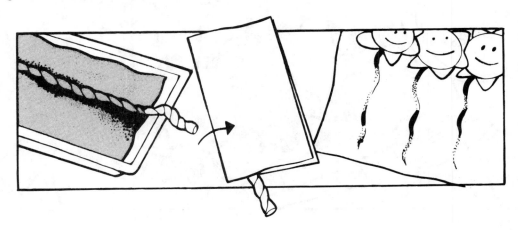

ART LESSON

Cow-Chalk Scenes— Moo! Moo!

★ Standards Check: Visual Arts

Materials

- ✓ buttermilk
- ✓ bowls
- ✓ paintbrushes
- ✓ dark construction paper
- ✓ pastel-colored chalk—some whole pieces and some broken in thirds

PROCEDURE

1. Place a small amount of buttermilk in bowls at the center.

2. Add paintbrushes, dark construction paper, and pastel-colored chalk.

3. Have children paint with the buttermilk to cover the paper.

4. Next, have children use the colored chalk to create scenes of their choice. Encourage them to draw with the tips of the whole pieces and draw with the sides of the smaller pieces to create various types of lines.

5. When children are finished, have them work with a partner to take turns describing their "cow-chalk" scenes.

Note: Buttermilk helps to prevent the chalk from rubbing off after the paper dries and makes the colors brighter.

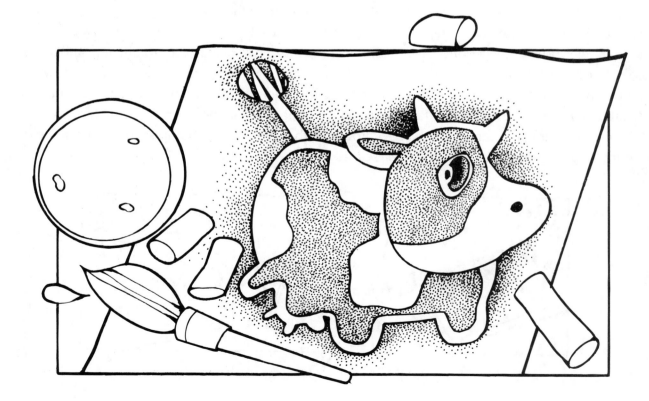

ART LESSON

Happy/Sad Watercolor Scenes

★ Standards Check: Visual Arts

Materials

✓ flower reproducible (page 90)
✓ two musical selections—one upbeat and the other slow and somber
✓ CD or tape player
✓ paintbrushes
✓ red, orange, and yellow paint
✓ blue, purple, brown, and black paint
✓ drying rack or clothesline with clothespins

PROCEDURE

1. Place the two musical selections in the center.

2. Remind children that art, like music, can convey a mood. As they listen to the happy music, have children paint a scene of their choice, or paint the flower, using only red, orange, and yellow paint.

3. Place the paintings on a drying rack or on a clothesline stretched across the center.

4. Later, invite children to listen to the slower, somber music. Have children paint a similar scene, or the flower, using only blue, purple, brown, and black.

5. Allow the paintings to dry. Have children compare the two scenes and talk about how each painting makes them feel.

Let's Create! at the MUSIC CENTER

TO KNOW

It is important to model any songs and movement techniques with the whole group prior to children working in centers. Provide enough space in the center so that children can sing and move safely. Whenever possible, have children use rhythm instruments and props to accompany creative movement with music and to help them internalize the rhythm of the music. Use the following suggestions to increase the success of enjoyable, developmentally appropriate sound and movement explorations during music center time.

Teaching a New Song

Use a variety of the following methods to help children gradually learn a new song and be ready to sing it enthusiastically during center time.

Model It: Select a song or chant. Sing or play the recording of the whole selection at tempo all the way through, since children need to hear language in its entirety. Then sing it all the way through, but sing it more slowly.

Echo Chant: Listen to the song in short segments and have children echo the words. Small portions are easier for children to store in short-term memory. Pick out familiar or repeated parts of the song (rhythm patterns), and cue children when it is time to join in with the music.

Call and Response: Sing one line of the song, and have children sing the next line. Continue in this way until you have sung the whole song.

Unison: Have children sing the whole song with you in unison.

Body Percussion: As you sing the song, include rhythmic taps, pats, or claps. By adding this movement, children are more actively involved with the song, so the learning is strengthened.

How Centers Help

Using centers to expose children to music helps develop their ability to listen for sound and rhythm, which are the essential components of music and speech. Children are more likely to hear sounds in words when they can listen for, identify, discriminate, and create sounds, sound patterns, rhythm, and rhythm patterns. These experiences will help develop children's phonological and phonemic awareness.

Adding Movement to Music

Adding movement activities to music is always a favorite with young children. There are two types of basic body movements. The first includes movements performed in a stationary position, such as pushing and pulling, swinging and swaying, twisting, turning, bending, rising up, or falling downward. The second includes movements that take a child from one place to another, such as walking, running, hopping, sliding, jumping, leaping, galloping, and skipping. Both types of basic body movements can be performed to the beat of the music and add fun and energy to the musical exploration.

It is important to adapt movements to the age of the children and to the special needs of individual class members. An excellent way to determine movement activities that are appropriate for your students is to first observe them at play. In this setting, children will use movements that are developmentally appropriate.

When initiating movement activities that you will encourage children to use on their own during center time, start by having each child find a space and remain in it during the movement exploration. Circles of yarn or string, hula hoops placed flat on the floor, or areas marked with chalk or tape can define each child's personal space. In time, remove the assigned spaces and have small groups of students take turns performing the movement activity for the class. In this way, young children will develop self-control, understand "my place in space," and be better prepared to enjoy their musical experiences during center time.

TO HAVE

Rhythm Instruments

✓ drums—coffee cans or oatmeal cylinders covered with colored paper and sealed with plastic tape

✓ rhythm sticks—painted wooden dowels, unsharpened pencils or chopsticks

✓ rhythm shakers—margarine tubs or plastic water bottles filled with rice, dried beans, aquarium gravel or sand, and sealed with plastic tape

✓ handbells—bells glued on tongue depressors

✓ wrist and ankle bells—bells sewn on elastic bands

Inexpensive Music Center Props

✓ long, silky scarves

✓ ribbons of various sizes tied to wooden dowels or unsharpened pencils

✓ crepe-paper streamers

✓ hula hoops

✓ peacock feathers

✓ hats or caps

✓ capes made from fabric scraps or towels

Other Materials

✓ CD players and musical CDs

✓ tape recorder

✓ cassette tapes—class-made and professionally recorded

✓ multicultural music and instruments

✓ classical music

✓ books to sing and read

Music Center Standards Chart

Musical Arts	The Singing Scarf	Washboard Band	String Action	Mirror Me!	Rah-Rah Boogie	Be the Wave	Sing-a-Song Bag
Sings simple familiar songs							●
Plays with a variety of musical instruments		●					
Echoes short rhythms and melodic patterns	●						
Responds to the tempo and rhythm of music	●	●	●	●	●	●	
Responds to music through purposeful movement	●	●	●	●	●	●	

TO DO CENTER IDEAS AND ACTIVITIES

The Singing Scarf

★ Standards Check: Musical Arts

The "Singing Scarf" is a fun vocal warm-up exercise. Put a silky, chiffon scarf on the floor. Ask the children to begin singing with a low "Ahhhhh" sound. Pick up the scarf and slowly lift it into the air. Have children slide their voices higher as the scarf is elevated. When the scarf is at its highest point, children are singing at their highest tone. Then, slowly and gradually lower the scarf to the ground as the children slide their voices downward to the beginning tone. In this way children will discover the full range of their voices. Encourage children to take turns leading the Singing Scarf during center time.

Washboard Band

★ Standards Check: Musical Arts

Recycle corrugated cardboard to create washboard instruments. Use a hole punch to place two holes in the top of a 9" x 12" piece of cardboard. Insert enough twine or yarn to create a strap that will allow the instrument to hang loosely on the chest of the performer. The corrugated part of the cardboard must be exposed in order to get a musical sound. Then, cut a 3-inch circular pick, and tie it to the instrument with another piece of yarn. Have children use markers to decorate their washboard instruments. Turn on a recording of rhythmic music, and have some children at the center ready to dance and other band members ready to play. Let the old-fashioned center time fun begin!

String Action

★ Standards Check: Musical Arts

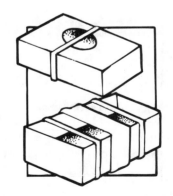

Let students create individual "guitars" using different-sized boxes and rubber bands of various colors and thicknesses. Have children stretch the bands over the open boxes and then pluck the "guitar strings" to investigate how the vibrations create sound. Ask children to think about questions such as *Do the strings on the long boxes sound like the strings on the shorter ones?* Or *What happens if you use skinny (or thick) rubber bands?*

Extension: Bring in a real guitar. Tighten and loosen the strings so children can hear the different tones. Talk about the different sounds the guitar makes. Have smooth flowing guitar music available for children to listen to as they join in with their own guitars.

Mirror Me!

★ Standards Check: Musical Arts

Place a full-length mirror in the music center. Add a CD or cassette player and a musical recording of soft, smooth flowing music. Let children practice making slow, sustained movements in front of the mirror as the music plays. Encourage them to carefully watch their mirrored image.

Variation: Pair children so that one child is the leader and the other is the "mirror." Play the music again, and let them try mirroring each other's slow-motion movements, taking turns being the leader and the mirror.

Rah-Rah Boogie

★ Standards Check: Musical Arts

Rah-rahs are miniature pom-poms. To make these, cut red and green tissue into one-inch wide colored tissue strips. Staple lots of red strips onto one tongue depressor and lots of green strips onto another tongue depressor. Place rah-rahs and boogie-woogie music in the center. Have children hold red rah-rahs in their right hands and green rah-rahs in their left hands. Have children alternate holding up their left and right hands, shaking the appropriate rah-rah while moving to the boogie-woogie beat.

Be the Wave

★ Standards Check: Musical Arts

Place classical or New Age music (music with added ocean sound effects also works well) and scarves or ribbon streamers in the center. Have children play the musical tape or CD on low volume and use the scarves and their arms to become the ocean waves ebbing and flowing with the sound of the music.

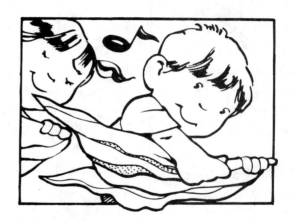

MUSIC LESSON

Sing-a-Song Bag

★ Standards Check: Musical Arts

Materials

- ✓ Old MacDonald props reproducibles (pages 97–98)
- ✓ Old MacDonald Had a Farm song sheet (page 99)
- ✓ tape recorder
- ✓ blank cassette tape
- ✓ crayons or markers
- ✓ scissors
- ✓ tape or glue
- ✓ lunch-size paper bags
- ✓ tongue depressors or craft sticks

PROCEDURE

1 Make a transparency of the "Old MacDonald" song sheet. Sing it with the children during circle time until they have memorized the words. Record the children singing the song. Place the tape in the center and complete Steps 2–5. Once children are familiar with the song, they are ready for this fun sing and sequence activity.

2 Duplicate enough copies of the barn setting and the song character props for the children at the center.

3 Have children color and cut out the barn and glue it to a lunch-size paper bag to create a "setting" for the song.

4 Next, have them color and cut out the song props and glue or tape each one to a craft stick.

5 Have children play their class-made tape on a low volume and use their displayed song props to sequence the verses by dropping the appropriate character into the bag while singing along with the tape.

Variation: Make a larger-size bag setting from an enlarged version of the barn, a grocery bag, and enlarged character props glued to paint sticks. Place all of the props inside the setting bag, and place it at the listening center.

Old MacDonald's Barn

Directions: Color the barn. Cut it out. Glue it to a paper lunch bag.

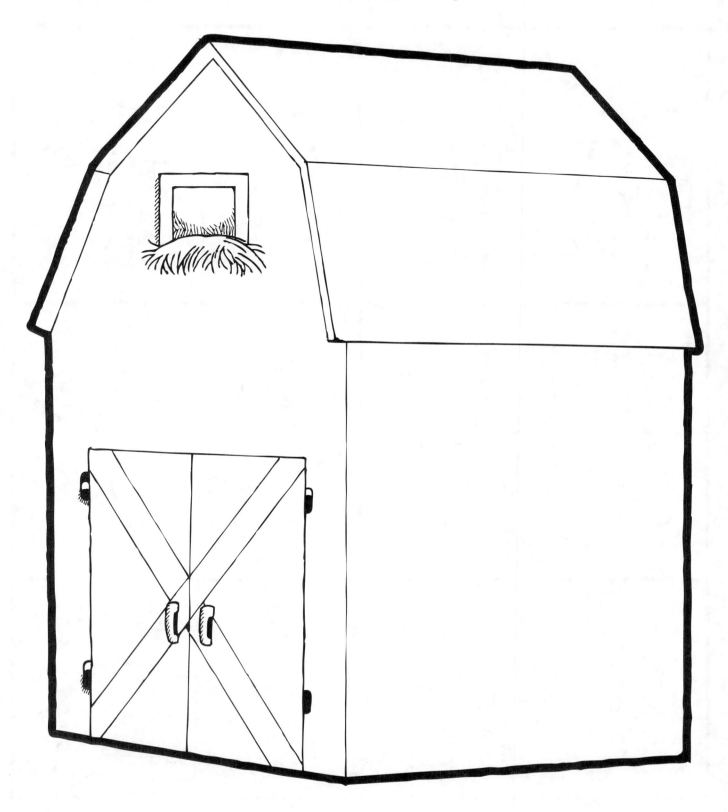

Old MacDonald Characters

Directions: Color the characters. Cut them out. Glue each character to a craft stick.

Early Childhood Centers © 2007 Creative Teaching Press

Old MacDonald Had a Farm

Old MacDonald had a farm,

E-I-E-I-O.

And on his farm he had a cow,

E-I-E-I-O.

With a moo, moo here,

And a moo, moo there,

Here a moo, there a moo,

Everywhere a moo, moo.

Old MacDonald had a farm,

E-I-E-I-O.

Pig—oink, oink
Duck—quack, quack
Dog—ruff, ruff

Literacy Centers

Introduction

Literacy centers provide an opportunity for all children to engage in meaningful, standards-based literacy-building activities that enrich their skill development and understanding. During literacy centers, the teacher works with small groups or individuals pulled from the various centers, or he or she can "be a center" that children visit.

Literacy centers may be open-ended or task specific. They provide children with ample opportunities to pretend read, begin to read, listen to taped stories and poems, or read along with such recordings. These centers provide time for children to draw pictures and then write about their drawings, and to speak and listen to their friends. Literacy centers reinforce existing alphabet/phonics instruction and language development programs. In prekindergarten and kindergarten, literacy centers support the development, review, or extension of the Reading First and Early First components. In addition, literacy centers in kindergarten support the learning happening in small-group or guided-reading time.

Literacy centers provide teachers with a meaningful way to differentiate experiences, accommodate different learning styles, and build children's self-esteem as they experience success. Literacy centers can evolve from your whole-group, small-group, and individual activities. For example, after reading a big book, place it in the big book center. After singing a song, place the taped version in the poetry and song center. This method of center development allows you to have center materials that children already know how to use. As a result, you will have more time to work uninterrupted with small groups or individuals.

Each of the following literacy center areas can contain several centers with multiple activities in each. These activities can be cumulative to provide children with unlimited chances to practice and master the skills. The following four literacy center areas should be considered in prekindergarten, and all or part of them should also be considered in kindergarten:

Let's Listen! —**Listening Post Center**

Let's Read! —**Reading Center**

Let's Learn Letters & Words! —**ABC and Word Work Center**

Let's Write! —**Writing and Illustrating Center**

 **at the LISTENING POST CENTER**

Children benefit from listening to familiar stories on tape, hearing nursery rhymes, and reading along with a recorded voice. They hear fluent reading with expression and attempt to make their voices sound exactly like the taped voice. In doing so, they begin to develop an ear for what expressive, fluent reading sounds like. Children also develop the ability to listen for rhyme, alliteration, and onomatopoeia as they listen to songs, chants, and poems. This helps children to develop phonemic awareness, a precursor to success in phonics instruction and reading ability.

How Centers Help

Centers provide children numerous listening activities to participate in within a given time. Many teachers find it helpful to have children use individual cassette players and CD players instead of all children "plugging in" to a common listening center device. That way, children can choose what they want to hear and when they want to hear it instead of having to follow along with a selection that may not interest them. In addition, it enables you to have a variety of centers open at the same time. Consider asking parents to lend individual cassette or CD players and headphones for the class to use during the school year.

TO HAVE

- ✔ individual CD players, tape players, headphones, and blank cassette tapes
- ✔ read-along books with cassettes or CDs
- ✔ crayons, markers, paper, and scissors
- ✔ story response journals
- ✔ "Magic" write-on, lift-off slates with stylus
- ✔ follow-the-directions tapes
- ✔ class-made songs, nursery rhymes, poems, and story tapes

- ✔ big books read by the whole class on tape
- ✔ classical music tapes
- ✔ multicultural music tapes with theme-specific or culture-specific stories
- ✔ camping chairs, beanbag chairs, carpet squares, and other comfy places to sit and listen
- ✔ rhythm band instruments

Listening Post Standards Chart

Listening and Speaking Skills	Name That Sound	We Made That!	The Hit Parade	The Hit Parade, Part 2	Sound-Effect Stories	Listen and Tell
Knows words are made up of sounds		●	●	●	●	●
Listens to a variety of genres		●	●		●	●
Listens for a variety of purposes	●	●	●		●	●
Knows the source of a variety of sounds	●			●	●	
Retells the sequence of a story		●		●	●	●

TO DO CENTER IDEAS AND ACTIVITIES

Name That Sound

★ Standards Check: Listening and Speaking Skills

Tape-record common school sounds and photograph someone or something making that sound. Place the tape in the center. Have children listen to the sound, turn off the tape player, find the photograph of the person or thing making the sound, and then continue the tape until all pictures have been matched to the taped sounds. Try the following fun examples: a child coughing, the school bell ringing, the toilet flushing, water running, the teacher sneezing, the principal saying *Good morning, boys and girls*, children playing on the playground, and a stack of blocks being knocked down.

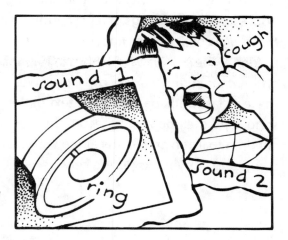

We Made That!

★ Standards Check: Listening and Speaking Skills

Tape-record the class reading a class-made book in which each child has made one page. Store the book and cassette in a resealable plastic bag. A fun book to make is one based on the old song "Mary Wore Her Red Dress." Read aloud *Mary Wore Her Red Dress*, adapted by Merle Peek, and have children write and illustrate pages about something they are wearing. Have the children sing their pages on tape. For example, *Dan wore his brown pants all day long, Dayton wore his black shoes all day long*, or *Mattie wore her pink ribbons all day long*.

The Hit Parade

★ Standards Check: Listening and Speaking Skills

Tape-record an assortment of age-appropriate favorite songs, poems, nursery rhymes, finger plays, or jump rope jingles to aid in teaching the selections to the class. Place the tapes along with the text in the listening center. Invite children to sing along with favorite songs and rhymes, move to the beat of the music or the rhythm of the words. For children who are ready, encourage them to follow the text as they listen.

The Hit Parade, Part 2

★ Standards Check: Listening and Speaking Skills

Another favorite activity is to read and sing along with picture books inspired by songs. A few charming examples are *Mama Don't Allow* by Thacher Hurd, *Cat Goes Fiddle-i-Fee* by Paul Galdone, *The Itsy, Bitsy Spider* by Iza Trapani, and *Skip to My Lou* and *Peanut Butter and Jelly* by Nadine Westcott. Have children make a class book based on the text of the picture book and song. Bind their book, and record them performing it. Invite children to listen and follow along with their own personalized songs and storybooks during centers.

★ Sound-Effect Stories

★ Standards Check: Listening and Speaking Skills

Read aloud a story with lots of action, such as *Too Much Noise* by Ann McGovern in which the bed creaks, the floor squeaks, and the leaves swish. Tape-record the story as you read it, and pause at each point in the story when a good sound-effect would be appropriate. Place the tape in the center and allow children to play it on a low volume and add the sound effects with their voices or rhythm band instruments at the appropriate time. Remind children to stop making the sound effect as soon as the story continues.

Listen and Tell

★ Standards Check: Listening and Speaking Skills

Invite children to listen to stories on cassette or CD. Create and place in the center a felt board along with the characters or items from the story, each backed with felt. Place the book, tape or CD, and storytelling props in a resealable plastic bag. After children hear the story, have them use the felt board and props to retell the story in their own words. Later, they can record their thoughts about the story on the Here's What I Think! reproducible (page 105).

Teacher Tip: Have parent volunteers or reading buddies help children with writing the date, title of the book, and the author. Or select one recorded book for everyone in the center to hear. That way, you can fill in the reproducible with the appropriate information before you duplicate it.

Name _____ Date _____

Here's What I Think!

Title _____

Author _____

I think this book is

Great

Okay

Not for me

Here is a picture from the story.

at the **READING CENTER**

Reading is a developmental process that children become more proficient at over time and with practice. Children need to read and be read to every day. Children need to use the background knowledge they bring to the reading experience, along with their vocabulary knowledge and their understanding of word order or grammar, to aid their ability to read independently.

To provide children with all they need to launch into the reading process, model reading with expression, read from all genres, and make materials available for children to "practice read" what has been read to them. Provide a comfortable area for quiet reading time in the library center. In addition, remember that reading does not occur just in books, so display charts, post directions and instructions with print and rebus drawings, and label objects in the classroom.

To read independently, children must conquer the alphabetic code. Hearing sounds in words is the basis of phonemic awareness and eventual sound/symbol recognition. Research supports that our brains seek patterns and relate to sound and rhythm patterns created by language and song. Short rhymes, songs, picture books, alphabet books, poetry, and patterned, predictable books use rhythm, rhyme, and repetition to help to teach sound/symbol connections, phonics, and invented spelling. In addition, they provide opportunities for responding to literature.

How Centers Help

The activities you place at centers will help children identify, reproduce, and create sounds and rhythms in a fun, game-like atmosphere to develop their reading skills and strategies. As children experience familiar literature, they listen to and speak the text and read, chant, or sing the words. Once modeled in large-group and small-group time, all of these activities and skills can be extended, practiced, and practiced again in developmentally appropriate ways until mastered during the literacy center time experience in the reading center.

Reading Stages

Children develop as readers in stages. The following section describes the characteristics and needs of our early- and upper-emergent readers in prekindergarten and kindergarten.

Stage	Emergent Reader Characteristics	Emergent Reader Needs
Emergent Reader	✓ Enjoys being read to and will often ask to hear the same story over and over ✓ Imitates reading-like behaviors learned from observing reading styles of teachers, parents, or siblings ✓ Begins to discover the connection between oral and written language ✓ Uses his or her own language to tell a story but "borrows" text from books previously read ✓ Begins to discover that he or she can read the same words in many different formats and books	✓ Print-rich environment where independent reading is scaffolded and encouraged ✓ Many opportunities to hear rich literature being read aloud by teachers, visitors, older children, and reading buddies or in tape-recorded stories ✓ Many opportunities to respond to literature in multimodal ways using rhythm, rhyme, art, music, and drama ✓ Participation in shared, modeled, and interactive reading and writing skill instruction should be systematic and explicit but should always focus on meaning and be connected to meaningful reading opportunities—songs, poems, chants, books, environmental print, and picture-noun (familiar words) word walls

TO HAVE

✓ tape recorder/player

✓ blank cassette tapes

✓ books, poems, and songs on tape

✓ pointers of various sizes, shapes, lengths, and themes

✓ "Super Specs"—play reading glasses in various sizes and shapes

✓ big books, magazines, newspapers, and picture books

✓ emergent-level books—fiction, nonfiction, and theme-related

✓ "comfy" pillows, chairs, and pads

✓ bookcases, boxes, and tubs

✓ small wading pool

✓ bookmarks

✓ StikkiClips

✓ letter/word hunt sticks (page 110)

✓ paper, pencils, crayons, markers, and glue

✓ construction paper, self-stick notes, index cards, and note pads

✓ computer and appropriate software programs

✓ songs and poem charts

✓ pocket chart with story, poem, and song sentence/word/picture strips

✓ magnetic board/flannel board with magnetic/flannel story characters/props

✓ picture/letter/word games and puzzles

✓ decorated book boxes for storing books by readability

Reading Center Standards Chart

Reading Skills and Strategies	Left-Right Chairs	Big Book Center	Poetry and Song Center	Pocket Chart Stories	Read-the-Room Center
Knows the difference between letters, numbers, and words					●
Knows print and written symbols convey meaning	●	●	●	●	
Understands pictures/illustrations convey meaning	●	●		●	
Knows the proper way to handle books	●	●		●	
Knows print is read from left to right, top to bottom, and front to back	●	●	●	●	
Knows letters of the alphabet					●
Knows familiar words in print		●	●		●
Uses emergent reading skills to "read" a story	●	●	●	●	
Knows books have titles, authors, and illustrators	●	●		●	
Uses pictures and print to aid comprehension		●	●	●	
Uses basic elements of phonetic analysis (to decode)		●	●	●	
Understands level-appropriate sight words and vocabulary		●	●	●	
Reads aloud familiar stories, poems, and songs	●	●	●	●	
Knows the sequence of events				●	

TO DO CENTER IDEAS AND ACTIVITIES

Left-Right Chairs

★ Standards Check: Reading Skills and Strategies

Help children improve reading fluency with this activity. Place two child-size chairs side by side and tie them together with a ribbon. Hang a pair of traced and decorated hands from the bow. Label the left hand *left-hand chair* and the right hand *right-hand chair*. For fun, paint the fingernails of the paper hands or place decals or glitter on them. Near the chairs place a container of familiar patterned and predictable books that children have memorized. Have two children hold each side of a selected book. Have the child on the right turn the pages. Have the child on the left read all left-hand pages and the child on the right read all right-hand pages. When the reading is complete, have children trade places and read the book again. The novelty of this activity will maintain children's interest.

Big Book Center

★ Standards Check: Reading Skills and Strategies

After reading a favorite big book during group time, place it in the center along with "super specs" and thematic pointers for children to take turns "being the teacher," while others act as the readers. For instance, if the book is about a pond, have the pretend teacher don a pair of specs and select from a variety of pointers with pond animal decals, cutouts, or foam shapes attached.

Poetry and Song Center

★ Standards Check: Reading Skills and Strategies

Place the text of favorite poetry and songs in decorated boxes or bins. Include famous works of poetry, nursery rhymes, and child-created poems. Place audio recordings of songs or poetry in the center for children to follow along with.

Pocket Chart Stories

★ Standards Check: Reading Skills and Strategies

Make a transparency or chart using the One, Two, Buckle My Shoe reproducible (page 111), or select another familiar poem or song. Teach the song to the children until it is almost memorized. Write the verses on sentence strips. Use cutout shapes or the rebus drawings on pages 112–113 to illustrate the lines of the verses on separate cards. Place the lines of text in the pocket chart in sequence. Have children read the familiar rhyme, line by line, point-tracking the text as modeled in whole-group time. Have children place the appropriate picture cards next to each line. Until prekindergarten children are ready for text, have them sequence the picture cards in the pocket chart and say the verse from memory.

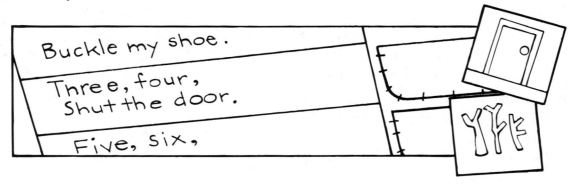

Read-the-Room Center

★ Standards Check: Reading Skills and Strategies

Place clipboards with colored copy paper, "cool" gel pens or scented markers, "super specs," and a set of letter or word cards with Letter/Word Hunt Sticks in the center. To make a Letter/Word Hunt Stick, glue a wiggly eye on the end of a paint paddle (paint stir stick) or tongue depressor. On the reverse side, behind the eye, affix a StikkiClip as shown. Letter/word cards can be easily added or removed from the clip. Have children don their selected "super specs," select a letter or word card, and clip it in the Letter/Word Hunt Stick. Have them track print on word walls, big books, or poem and song charts to spy the target letter or word. When the text is found, children use their cool pens or markers to attempt to write the letter or word on the clipboard. Remember to include a decorated stick, or magic wand, to make fun pointers for reading the room.

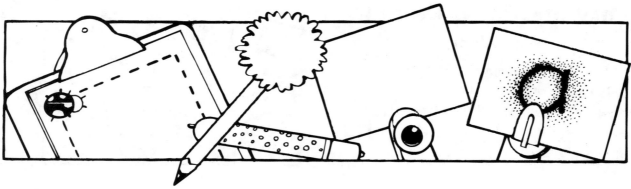

One, Two, Buckle My Shoe

One, two,
Buckle my shoe.

Three, four,
Shut the door.

Five, six,
Pick up sticks.

Seven, eight,
Lay them straight.

Nine, ten,
A big fat hen.

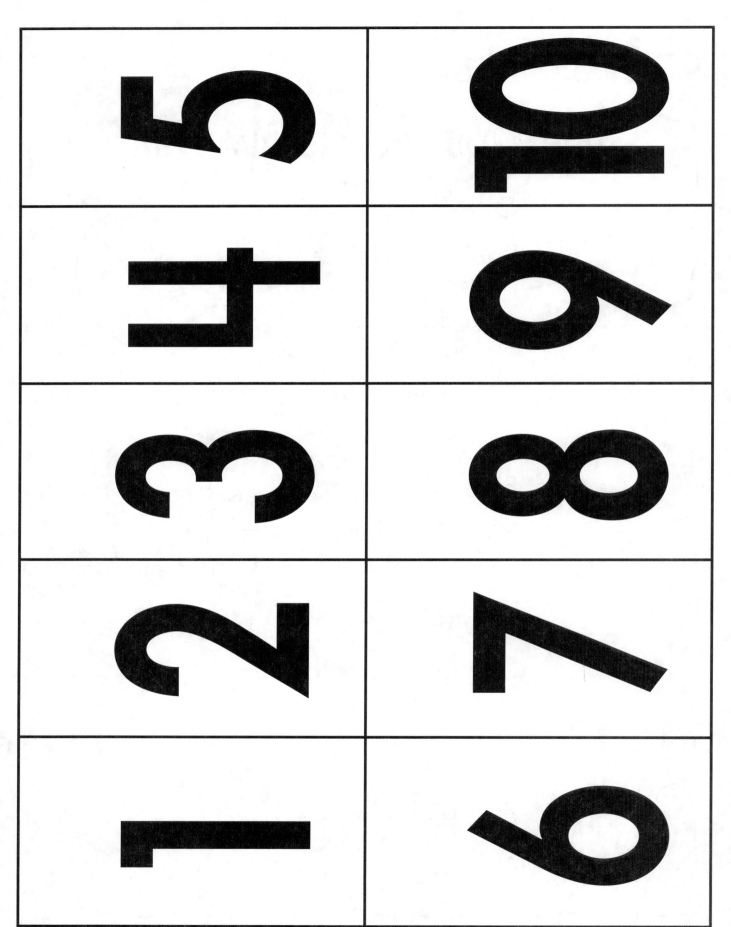

Early Childhood Centers © 2007 Creative Teaching Press

One, Two Buckle My Shoe Rebus Cards

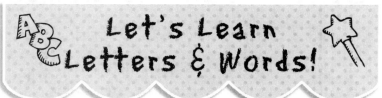

at the **ABC AND WORD WORK CENTER**

TO KNOW

The ABC and word work center helps to develop phonemic and phonological awareness, facilitate letter and word recognition, and enhance phonics instruction. **Phonemic awareness** is the knowledge that each word is made up of specific sounds, and **phonological awareness** is the ability to manipulate the sounds of language. For children to develop these skills, they need repeated opportunities to listen to and play with language. Young children are ready for **phonics** or sound/letter pairing when they have some phonemic and letter awareness and can recognize a core of consonants. Letter/word recognition is critical to both the reading and writing processes. Letter/word awareness activities help children quickly recognize specific letters and words and develop their automaticity and fluency. Research supports the need for children to master basic skills at the automaticity level so they can focus on their comprehension of what they read.

Jingles, chants, and dramatizations increase recall, especially for English-language learners and dyslexic children. Avoid rule-laden program activities in which children memorize and then recall rules on demand to facilitate word recognition. The human brain functions as a pattern detector rather than as a rule memorizer and implementer. Young children's work in phonics should begin with basic elements, such as sound/letter matching, and gradually move into more complex and subtle elements.

How Centers Help

Children in the ABC and word work center practice the alphabet, play with letter and sound associations, learn words that are common and important in their lives, and begin to create an awareness of high frequency words in a relaxed, risk-free atmosphere through games, songs, and fun activities. Center opportunities provide greater levels of practice than possible in the whole-group setting, meaning that children have more chances to develop their own understanding. Further, the center practice experiences provide children with multiple chances to use what they have learned in meaningful ways.

TO HAVE

- ✓ letter cards—capital and lowercase sets
- ✓ alphabet stamps and stamp pads
- ✓ self-stick notes
- ✓ tongue depressors and paint paddles (paint stir sticks)
- ✓ magnetic letters and magnetic boards
- ✓ pencils, crayons, markers, staplers, and glue
- ✓ construction paper, index cards, and note pads
- ✓ lined and unlined paper
- ✓ assortment of file folder, box, and plastic bag alphabet games
- ✓ alphabet puzzles
- ✓ picture-noun cards
- ✓ thematic illustrated word charts
- ✓ portable or individual "word wall" folders

ABC and Word Work Center Standards Chart

Reading and Writing Skills & Strategies	Letter Rubbings	Roll On	Print-Friendly	Menthol Fresh Letters	Letter Mosaics	Letter Patterns	Magic Letter	Touch, See, and Say Tray	Paper Plate Match-Up	Which Bin?	Letter Treasure Chest	Word Sort Time
Knows letters of the alphabet	●	●	●	●	●	●	●	●	●		●	●
Understands pictures/illustrations convey meaning			●	●					●	●	●	
Knows print and written symbols convey meaning			●					●			●	●
Uses phonetic knowledge	●	●	●	●	●		●	●	●	●		●
Uses forms of emergent writing				●								●

TO DO CENTER IDEAS AND ACTIVITIES

Letter Rubbings

★ Standards Check: Reading and Writing Skills & Strategies

Take one set of alphabet cards, and trace each letter with glue. Allow the glue to dry. Have children at the center place newsprint sheets on top of the alphabet cards and rub them with the sides of unwrapped, broken jumbo crayons. Magically, the letters are revealed! Invite children to trace the letters with their fingers as they say each letter's name or make its sound.

Roll On

★ Standards Check: Reading and Writing Skills & Strategies

Write large capital letters on individual paper plates. Make an identical set of letters on small cards. Have one child at the center be the "caller." The caller places the letter cards facedown in a pool. Have all other children at the center select one paper plate. When the caller draws a letter from the pool and says its name, the child with that plate stands and rotates the plate in a circle. As the child spins the plate around, the rest of the children quietly sing the song to the right to the tune of "The Farmer in the Dell." Have children in the center work together to name as many things as they can that start with the sound of the identified letter. The game continues until all cards have been drawn and all plates have been rolled and identified.

The S is rolling around.
The S is rolling around.
As soon as the letter S stops,
Name something that
starts with its sound.

Print-Friendly

★ Standards Check: Reading and Writing Skills & Strategies

Ask children to bring in environmental print from food boxes and packages such as cake mixes, crackers, cereals, toothpaste, and drink mixes. Cut the front panel from the package, and place it in a transparency sleeve. Store the sleeves in a three-ring binder. Select or create a set of small-size letter cards representing any target alphabet letters previously introduced. Have children choose a letter card and place it in a Letter/Word Hunt Stick (page 110). Invite children to "hunt" for that letter on each piece of environmental print in the binder.

Menthol Fresh Letters

★ Standards Check: Reading and Writing Skills & Strategies

Write a few target letters on index cards, and place them in a pocket chart at the center. Squirt menthol shaving cream in a plastic or metal tray. Have each child select one letter from the chart and write it in the shaving cream as he or she says the letter's name or sound. When ready to try a different letter, have children take three fingers and smear the foam again to start over. Remind children to keep their hands away from their faces during this activity and to clean their hands immediately after completion.

Letter Mosaics

★ Standards Check: Reading and Writing Skills & Strategies

Read aloud to the class a fun alphabet story, such as *On Market Street* by Arnold Lobel. Each week, place large (6"–8") tagboard letters and a variety of collage materials in the center. Have children design their own mosaic letters using the materials. For example, the letter "A" could be decorated with apple seeds, "B" could have buttons, and "C" could have cotton balls. Or have children cut out magazine pictures that begin with the letter sounds. Over time, after all the letters have been introduced to the class, and A to Z are finished, have children who come to the center take the letters, line them up in order on the floor, and sing the alphabet song. Or bind the pages into a class-made alphabet book.

Letter Patterns

★ Standards Check: Reading and Writing Skills & Strategies

Place alphabet stamps, various color stamp pads, and tagboard strips in the center. Have children select two or three stamps to create an alphabet pattern card. When the cards are finished, children work with partners to read the two- or three-member patterns and tell which letter would come next. For example, in the pattern APB, APB, AP, "B" would be next.

Variation: For prekindergarten children, place premade alphabet pattern cards at the center for them to finish.

Magic Letter

★ Standards Check: Reading and Writing Skills & Strategies

Invite children to explore substituting sounds in words with this word play center. Create a set of letter cards, and place the card with the focus letter on a small tabletop easel. It now becomes the "Magic Letter." Place one set of name cards in the center. Have children at the center take the class name cards and place them facedown in a pool. Have each child at the center draw a card, identify the name, and then say it again by substituting the real beginning sound with the Magic Letter's sound. For example, on "Magic M" day, children would change *Sara* to *Mara*, *Pablo* to *Mablo*, or *Jeremy* to *Meremy*. The game continues until all of the name cards have been made "magic." For prekindergarten, glue a picture to the children's name cards for quick identification.

Teacher Tip: Be sure to run through all of the names with the "Magic Letter" of the week to identify any possibilities of inappropriate language or name-calling.

Touch, See, and Say Tray

★ Standards Check: Reading and Writing Skills & Strategies

Cover the bottom of foam trays with aluminum foil. Cut to fit, and glue the foil to the tray. Cover the tray with a thin coating of salt. Remind children not to eat the salt or rub it in their eyes. Place a small set of letter cards in the center. Children select a card and practice writing it in the salt tray with their fingertips. As they write in the salt, the shiny foil appears. Encourage children to say the name of the letter as they write it. For children who are ready, place word cards in the center.

Paper Plate Match-up

★ Standards Check: Reading and Writing Skills & Strategies

Cut 26 inexpensive, flat paper plates in half. On each top half, write a capital letter of the alphabet. Cut the bottom halves in half. On each bottom left quarter write a lowercase letter, and on each bottom right quarter glue a picture that begins with the letter's sound. When choosing pictures for the vowel letters, use short vowel sound pictures. Place the pieces for six to seven alphabet letters in resealable plastic bags to create various sets to play with (26 plates in a bag are too many pieces to manage). To play the game, have children sort the pieces into capital letters, lowercase letters, and pictures. Then have children select the top pieces and lay them out on the floor. Ask children to find the matching lowercase letter pieces and matching picture-sound pieces to complete the paper plate match-ups.

Which Bin?

★ Standards Check: Reading and Writing Skills & Strategies

Select target letters, and collect a plastic bin for each one. Make a set of alphabet cards to match the target letters, and use transparent tape to attach each card to a bin. Ask children to bring in toys and other small objects that begin with the target sounds, for example, *pig, penny,* or *purse* for *p*. Randomly arrange the objects for all target sounds at the center, and place the bins in a row. Have children select objects, identify them, say the beginning sound, and place them in the appropriate letter bins. Invite children to repeat this process until all objects are in the appropriate containers. Add new letter bins each week, or just add one more each week, and remove the letters children have mastered.

Variation: For a higher-level activity, have children sort by ending sounds.

can use sorting tray

Teacher Tip: Photograph the items for each letter and place each photo underneath the matching container in order for children to self-check their work.

Letter Treasure Chest

★ Standards Check: Reading and Writing Skills & Strategies

Create a "treasure chest" by using glue to attach colorful craft supplies such as beads, sequins, tissue paper, and ribbon to a box. Place alphabet blocks with selected target letters in the treasure chest. Let children know that these blocks are the "treasure." Place the chest along with various alphabet books at the center. Have children select a treasure from the chest, identify a letter on one of the block's faces and find the matching letter page in an alphabet book. Once they find the matching page, have children name all of the pictures on the page that start with the treasure letter.

Word Sort Time

★ Standards Check: Reading and Writing Skills & Strategies

Select common or high frequency words from the word wall and write each word on a small index card. Or use children's names. Copy the Word Sort T reproducible (page 121), laminate it, and place it in the center with the word or name cards. Each time children visit the center, change the categories on the T chart. For example, one week the two categories could be *words with the letter a* and *words without the letter a*. Another week the categories could be *words with 3 letters* and *words with more than 3 letters*.

Word Sort

Words with the letter a	Words without the letter a
Hannah	Ben
Dallas	Jeremy
Gabe	Dominque
David	
Nicholas	

Word Sort

Words with three letters	Words with more than 3 letters
cat	this
the	what
boy	girl
sat	

Word Sort

Left column and right column with header lines, divided by a vertical line.

 **Let's Write!** at the **WRITING AND ILLUSTRATING CENTER**

TO KNOW

Writing is about communication. Being able to share one's ideas through drawings and writing is a powerful and motivating experience for children. Writing is a developmental process that children become more proficient at over time and with practice. Children's initial attempts are often through drawings, but in time they progress to include words and sentences. It is important to children's academic development and self-esteem to value every stage of the process.

Children need opportunities to express themselves through writing every day, from the first day of school to the last! Provide children with a variety of writing experiences to support the following writing stages and help scaffold their learning.

Children tend to first communicate through their drawings. (1)

Next, children often add scribbles to imitate writing they see. (2)

Then, children begin to elongate their scribbles into character-like and letter-like formations. (3)

Then, children begin to create letter strings. (4)

Often, children will use their developing knowledge of sound-symbol correspondence to label their drawings. (5)

And last, they write so that others can begin to read their messages. (6)

How Centers Help

Developmentally appropriate activities enrich children's writing skills and provide them with a desire to write and communicate with others. During center time, children can write names, lists, notes, stories, poems, and songs. They can create labels for their drawings, art projects, and block constructions. Children can also write letters to family members and friends, make name place cards for creative dramatics, create menus, and take pretend restaurant food orders.

Writing Stages

Children develop their writing skills at various rates. The following chart describes the characteristics and needs of early-emergent and upper-emergent writers in prekindergarten and kindergarten.

Stage	Emergent Writer Characteristics	Emergent Writer Needs
Emergent Writer	✓ Draws pictures to write stories. ✓ Uses scribbling, symbol writing, or letter strings in early writing attempts. ✓ Understands that talk can be written down, but may not understand how the process works. ✓ Begins to use left-to-right directional movement. ✓ Often "tells" his or her writing to others to "read" it. ✓ Begins to develop phonemic awareness and letter recognition skills, and begins to use those skills to invent spellings, especially with consonants. ✓ Begins to participate in frame or structured writing, using common syntax patterns or frames for his or her writing. ✓ Begins to choose his or her own writing topics.	✓ Many opportunities to hear literature from all genres read aloud to develop writing models and structures. ✓ Opportunities to dictate experiences to see their oral language in print. ✓ Daily opportunities to hear songs, poems, and chants as models for writing. ✓ Numerous whole- and small-group modeled and shared writing opportunities. ✓ Daily opportunities to self-select topics, write, and share writing. ✓ Instruction on phonemic awareness and letter recognition skills. ✓ Variety of writing instruments and papers, including unlined for prekindergarten and lined and unlined for kindergarten.

TO HAVE

- ✓ lined and unlined paper
- ✓ paper in all colors, sizes, textures, and shapes
- ✓ greeting cards, postcards, stationery "junk mail," and nonpersonalized checks and deposit slips
- ✓ various types of markers, pens, pencils, crayons, colored pencils, and chalk
- ✓ blank shape books
- ✓ typewriter and computer station

- ✓ letter- and legal-size envelopes
- ✓ alphabet cards, alphabet stamps, character stamps, and stamp pads
- ✓ clipboards
- ✓ class or theme-related word banks—be sure each word is illustrated with a rebus drawing
- ✓ stickers, stencils, and cutout shapes
- ✓ alphabet, sight word, and color word reference charts
- ✓ individual writing folders

Writing and Illustrating Center Standards Chart

Writing Skills and Strategies	Clay Snake Letters	Clay Dough Story Starter	Writing Folder Station	Shape Book Stories	Character Stamp Stories	My Draw and Tell News Journal	Developing Journals	The "Once Upon a Time" Story Box	"Thumb-Body" Special
Knows pictures and writing communicate meaning and information		●	●	●	●	●	●	●	●
Uses drawing to express ideas			●	●	●	●	●	●	
Dictates stories, poems, and personal narratives		●						●	
Knows letters of the alphabet	●		●						
Uses knowledge of letters to write or copy familiar words			●			●		●	●
Uses emergent writing skills		●	●	●	●	●	●	●	
Applies rudimentary rules of grammar		●		●	●	●	●	●	●
Uses phonetic knowledge		●		●	●	●	●	●	●
Uses conventions of print		●		●	●	●	●	●	●
Knows sequence of events				●	●		●	●	
Knows elements that compose a story				●	●			●	
Uses descriptive words to convey ideas				●	●		●	●	●

TO DO CENTER IDEAS AND ACTIVITIES

Clay Snake Letters

★ Standards Check: Writing Skills and Strategies

Prepare one of the dough recipes (page 130) in advance for this center activity. Place large laminated alphabet cards and plastic knives at the center. Have children roll the dough into "clay snakes" to support fine motor development. Next, have children cut the clay snakes into pieces to place onto the straight and curved lines of the letters to form them. Then, invite children to trace the clay dough letters with their fingertips. Provide unlined paper and crayons for children who are ready to try to write the letters on paper.

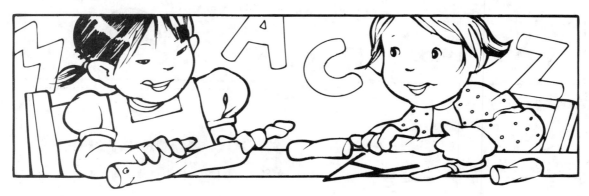

Clay Dough Story Starter

★ Standards Check: Writing Skills and Strategies

Stock the center with Make-It-Yourself Dough (page 130), old laminated charts turned over to use as dough work mats, cookie cutters, rolling pins, unlined paper, pencils, markers, and crayons. Have children roll out the dough and use cookie cutters to cut the dough into various shapes and characters. Challenge them to use the figures in stories they draw and tell about, or write about, depending on their levels of development.

Writing Folder Station

★ Standards Check: Writing Skills and Strategies

Have children create writing folders to store their writing samples. Give each child a two-pocket portfolio with prongs, and have children decorate the cover using stickers, stamps, gel pens, glitter pens, or puffy paint pens. Gluing a favorite photograph from home on the front cover is a fun way for children to personalize their folders and make it easier for them to find their own folders in the storage box.

Shape Book Stories

★ Standards Check: Writing Skills and Strategies

Use blank books shaped like apples, cars, or bears to inspire children's writing. Have children write fun stories or fun facts about apples, cars, or bears using their emergent writing skills.

Character Stamp Stories

★ Standards Check: Writing Skills and Strategies

Invite children to stamp scenes on pieces of drawing paper. Have children write stories based on the scenes they created. Or have children describe their scenes or label their pictures.

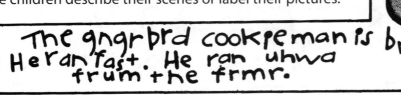

My Draw and Tell News Journal

★ Standards Check: Writing Skills and Strategies

Staple blank sheets of paper together with a construction paper cover to create a journal for each child. Have children attach a copy of the My Draw and Tell News Journal reproducible (page 131) to their covers. This type of journal provides children of all learning levels with an opportunity to view themselves as writers because they can draw pictures as a form of written communication and then talk about their drawings. As children learn about letter and sound connections, encourage them to label their pictures with letter strings, words, phrases, and then sentences. Have children write about exciting events in their lives that they would normally share during daily news or sharing circle times. They may write about something happening in their neighborhood, positive news at home, family events, birthdays, something they saw on television, or just any news they wish to share with other children in their center.

Developing Journals

★ Standards Check: Writing Skills and Strategies

Stock the writing center with journals made from construction paper covers and blank sheets of paper for children to write on. Vary the type of journal from week to week. Journals may be theme specific, such as *My Ocean Journal;* story time specific for responding to literature; or content specific, such as *My Math Journal* or *My Science Learning Log*. Have children draw, use stickers, rubber stamps and stamp pads, or cutout shapes, and include as much print as they can generate to describe their learning. Have children take their journals home at the end of each week, or use them periodically over time and send them home when completed.

WRITING LESSON

The "Once Upon a Time" Story Box

★ Standards Check: Writing Skills and Strategies

Materials

✓ decorated crate or special box labeled *The Once Upon a Time Story Box*

✓ story props such as a ball, toy drum, dolls, stuffed animals, magic wand, and a magic hat

PROCEDURE

1. After modeling for children how to use the items in the *Once Upon a Time* box to make up a story, place the storytelling activity in the center with the Story Box.

2. Have children take turns using as many of the Story Box items as they choose to make up and tell a story that always begins with, "Once upon a time…"

Variations:

1. **Theme-Specific Stories**
   Place items in the box from a current theme to encourage children to tell a story based on the topic of study.

2. **Tape-Recorded Stories**
   Tape-record the children making up and sharing their stories. Place the tape in the listening center for others to enjoy. This is especially helpful for prekindergarten children.

3. **Write-Your-Own Story**
   For a higher-level activity, have children tell the story and then display the selected props to inspire the writing of their stories. Invite children to use word banks, the word wall, and invented spelling to write their own versions of *Once Upon a Time...*

WRITING LESSON

"Thumb-Body" Special

★ Standards Check: Writing Skills and Strategies

Materials

✓ colored and white copy paper
✓ stapler
✓ stamp pads
✓ towelettes or moistened paper towels
✓ markers, crayons, or colored pencils

PROCEDURE

1. Ahead of time, prepare enough five-page step books for each child in the center. To make a step book, take one colored piece of copy paper, and layer two additional white pieces on top of it, about an inch apart from each other. Fold the top part over and down so that it looks like steps. Staple the booklet together. This makes a colored cover for the title, four white step pages, and a bottom color step for a five-part frame.

2. Write the following frame on each book for prekindergarten children. Write the frame on a chart for kindergarten children to copy into their own books.
   On each of the four white pages write, *I can_____.*
   On the last page write, *I am _____, "thumb-body" special!*

3. Place the step books in the center. Have children think of four things they can do well. Have prekindergarten children dictate to a parent volunteer or a teacher what they are good at. In kindergarten, have children use their sound-symbol knowledge to write as much as possible with invented spelling. In prekindergarten and kindergarten, have children write their own names on the last line. For example, *I am Jeremy, "thumb-body" special!*

4. After the frame text is written, have each child use the stamp pad to ink his or her thumb and place it on all five pages. After toweling thumbs clean, invite children to use markers, crayons, or colored pencils to show their thumb-bodies doing the activities described in the text.

5. When books are completed, have children practice reading their "Thumb-Body Special" stories to one another.

Make-It-Yourself Dough

Recipe #1

1 cup baking soda

½ cup cornstarch

½ cup water

(add food coloring, if desired)

Mix soda, cornstarch, and water in a saucepan. Cook and stir over low heat until mixture thickens. Cool on waxed paper and knead dough until smooth. Store unused dough in a resealable plastic bag in a cool place.

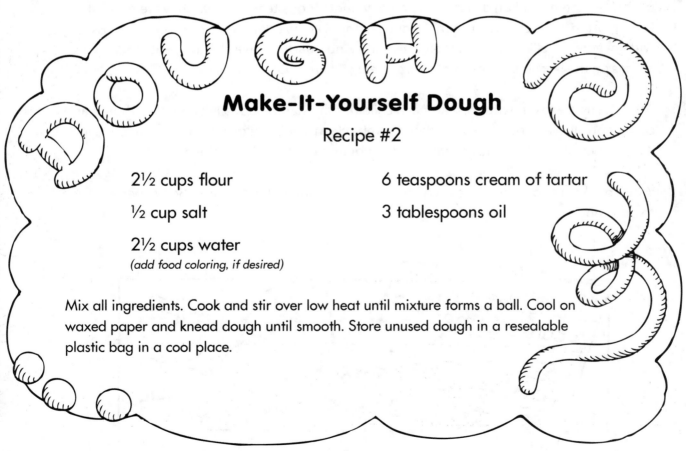

Make-It-Yourself Dough

Recipe #2

2½ cups flour

½ cup salt

2½ cups water
(add food coloring, if desired)

6 teaspoons cream of tartar

3 tablespoons oil

Mix all ingredients. Cook and stir over low heat until mixture forms a ball. Cool on waxed paper and knead dough until smooth. Store unused dough in a resealable plastic bag in a cool place.

My Draw and Tell News Journal

By _____

Theme Centers

Introduction

During a theme, materials are placed in all center areas that are not as generic as previously described, but very specific and tied directly to the theme. Theme centers can be useful as you develop and extend core knowledge in a unit of study during children's explorations. Theme centers incorporate all of the center types introduced in developmental and literacy centers.

Theme centers may occur every week, every month, or whenever a special interest develops. How often you plan to incorporate themes into your classroom is up to you and your students. The following section includes tips and graphic organizers to use when planning a theme and activity ideas for incorporating centers into a sample theme.

Planning a Theme

A theme is taught over time. It may consist of one unit of study that is multi-day or week-long, but often a theme may have several units that are all tied together. Study your curriculum objectives and standards to determine what you will cover in your theme. Then look at your available materials, and the activities you want children to participate in, to decide which are better suited to whole-group instruction at circle time or language and literacy time, and which would be better suited to small-group or individual participation. Integrate the small-group or individual activities into your center time. Keep noisier, more active choices for developmental centers and use activities that address literacy skills for the less active, more focused literacy centers.

Store all materials for a theme together in one area of the room or in one container. Place each unit of study in a folder, in its own jumbo resealable plastic bag, or in snap-on lid containers that can be stacked when not in use.

When planning a theme or unit of study, a graphic organizer is helpful. The organizers on the following pages will help you to plan your theme, select the standards that you will address, designate objectives to be accomplished by the children, gather your materials, and create an overview of what you hope to achieve through the theme. Remember, these organizers are meant to help you with your theme preparation, not to be more paperwork. After you use these for a while, you will be able to do the planning in your head. It will become natural. Even at this point, however, you may still choose to complete selected sections of the organizers to have something on paper for documentation.

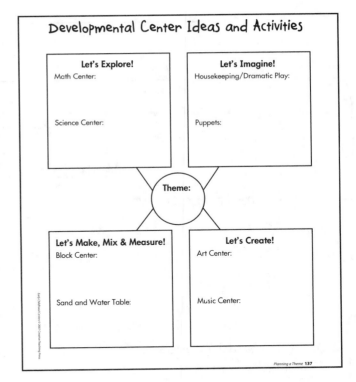

Use the Big Picture Planner on pages 134–136 to plan for the goals of your overall theme. Use the developmental center and literacy center webs on pages 137–138 to record specific activities and what you want children to accomplish in each of the centers. Use the Center Planning Sheet on page 139 for each new center you add to demonstrate how you are connecting your students' activities to the standards and curriculum objectives.

The "Big Picture" Theme Planner

Theme _____

Units of study _____

Standards _____

_____

Objectives _____

_____

Materials and Activities

Songs/Poems/Finger Plays   Big Books

Storybook Read-Alouds   Cooking/Special Events

Early Childhood Centers © 2007 Creative Teaching Press

The "Big Picture" Theme Planner, Page 2

Theme _____

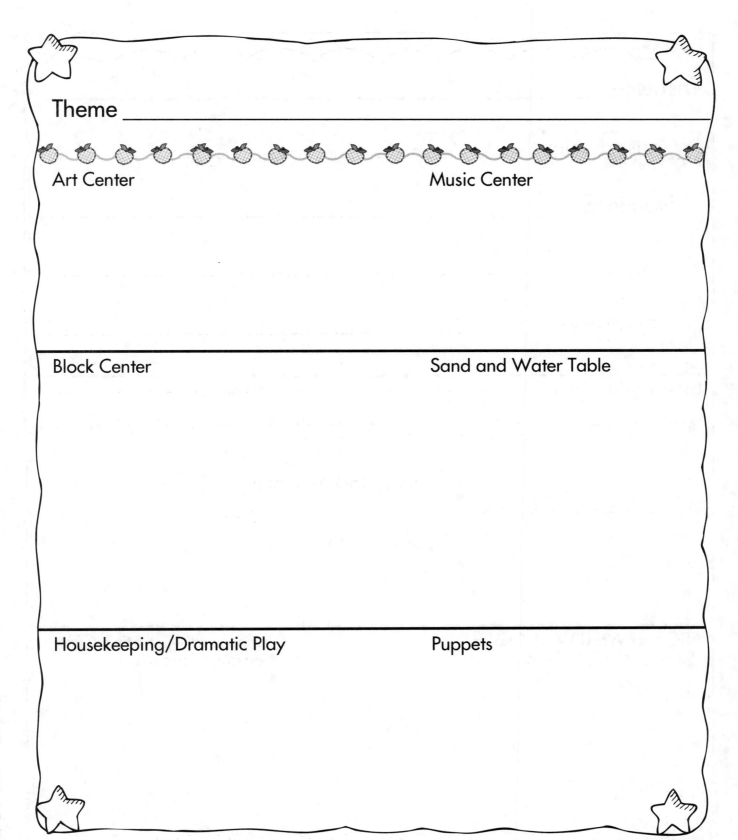

Art Center

Music Center

Block Center

Sand and Water Table

Housekeeping/Dramatic Play

Puppets

Theme _____

Math Center

Science Center

Listening Post Center

Reading Center

ABC and Word Work Center

Writing and Illustrating Center

Developmental Center Ideas and Activities

Let's Explore!

Math Center:

Science Center:

Let's Imagine!

Housekeeping/Dramatic Play:

Puppets:

Theme:

Let's Make, Mix & Measure!

Block Center:

Sand and Water Table:

Let's Create!

Art Center:

Music Center:

Literacy Center Ideas and Activities

Let's Listen!
Listening Post Center:

Let's Read!
Reading Center:

Theme:

Let's Learn Letters & Words!
ABC and Word Work Center:

Let's Write!
Writing and Illustrating Center:

Center Planning Sheet

Area:_____

Center:_____

Standards:_____

_____

Objectives:_____

_____

Materials:_____

_____

Description or Photograph of the Center

TO KNOW

Sample Theme: Our Growing and Changing World—Fall

- ✓ fiction and nonfiction books related to the theme
- ✓ *Look What I Did With a Leaf!* by Morteza E. Sohi (Walker Publishing Company, Inc., 1993)
- ✓ songs about fall
- ✓ magnifying glasses
- ✓ large piece of colored felt
- ✓ collections of fall leaves and twigs
- ✓ rubber stamps, stickers, cutout shapes, and stencils with a fall theme
- ✓ pumpkins and apples—both artificial and real
- ✓ large cardboard apple tree with twisted paper branches
- ✓ scale

TO DO CENTER IDEAS AND ACTIVITIES

The following set of sample center ideas and activities shows you how a fall unit can be integrated into various centers in your classroom. Use this general format as a guide to create centers for any unit or theme your class is studying.

Dramatic Play Center

Encourage children to bring straw "farm hats" from home. Use Velcro to attach red, yellow, and green apple cutout shapes to a cardboard tree with twisted paper branches. Have children pretend to be farmers harvesting their apple crop. Invite children to store their crop in "bushel baskets" and take them to market (the math center).

Math Center

After the harvest in the dramatic play area yields an apple crop, have children in the math center select their favorite kinds of apples and graph them onto a piece of felt (so the Velcro on the apples will adhere). When they are finished, have children display their graph, interpret the results, and report their findings orally or with pictures and writing in their math journals. Or have children use the apple cutout shapes to create two- or three-member patterns on felt, copy those patterns onto sentence strips and identify the patterns.

Science Center

Place an assortment of real red, yellow, and green apples for children to observe, weigh, smell, and taste in the center. Encourage them to talk about similarities and differences in the apples. Ask questions such as *Does the color make a difference in how it tastes?* or *Does the color determine the shape?* Have children collect the seeds to determine if all apples have the same kind of seeds regardless of color or shape. Have children study the seeds under a magnifying glass. Place a real pumpkin in the center for children to compare to the apples. Ask questions such as *How are they the same?* and *How are they different?* With assistance, children can write their comparison findings on a Venn diagram.

Housekeeping Center

After the apples are studied in the science center, wash them well and add them to the cooking area of the housekeeping center. With adult supervision, the center "family" can don aprons, gather cooking utensils, and make applesauce. You may want to try the recipe provided on the right.

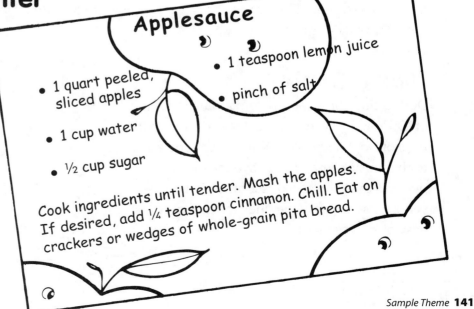

Applesauce

- 1 quart peeled, sliced apples
- 1 cup water
- ½ cup sugar
- 1 teaspoon lemon juice
- pinch of salt

Cook ingredients until tender. Mash the apples. If desired, add ¼ teaspoon cinnamon. Chill. Eat on crackers or wedges of whole-grain pita bread.

Block Center

Add small baskets of cutout fall leaves and plastic pumpkins and apples in the center. Have children load their crops on the block center vehicles and pretend to drive their loads to the market square, created with blocks by the children.

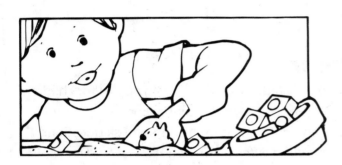

Sand Table

Hide brown linking cube "acorns" in the sand. Place squirrel face stickers or cutout shapes on the sand table scoops or on the handles of the scoops. Invite children to pretend to be squirrels digging for food. Provide a bucket for them to collect their acorns.

Art Center

Read aloud *Look What I Did With a Leaf!* by Sohi. Place it in the art center along with baskets of fall cutout leaves in various colors, shapes, and sizes. Have children arrange and glue the leaves on construction paper to create their own leaf creatures, leaf animals, leaf boys, or leaf girls. When the glue is dry, ask children to draw background scenery. Display their leaf art in an "art gallery" on the wall.

Music Center

During circle time tape-record a class rendition of "Do You Know the Fall Leaf Man?" sung to the tune of *Do You Know the Muffin Man?* and add it to the music center. Then have the group perform the song as a question and response song. Have boys ask the question and girls answer, or vice versa.

Do you know the fall leaf man,
The fall leaf man, the fall leaf man?
Oh, do you know the fall leaf man
Who lives on _____(name of school's street) Lane!

Yes, we know the fall leaf man,
The fall leaf man, the fall leaf man.
Why, yes, we know the fall leaf man
Who lives on _____Lane.

ABC and Word Work Center

Create fall word bags to read and reread. Make a *My Fall Words* rebus chart with the children during language and literacy time. Place the rebus chart, brown paper lunch bags, index cards, stamps and stamp pads, and stickers in the center. Have children color the top of the bag to look like a tree. Invite them to stamp apples or fall colored leaves on the treetop. Have prekindergarten children stamp a fall symbol, place a sticker, glue a fall cutout shape, or trace a stencil onto the index cards. Have kindergarten children copy the fall words onto one side of the index cards and illustrate the other side. Then, have younger children work with adult volunteers to say the name of each fall item and identify its beginning sound. Have older children practice reading the words.

FALL WORDS

acorn

apple

hat

leaf

pumpkin

scarecrow

Reading Center

Copy the "Apple-Pickin' Time" poem (on the right) onto a chart or sentence strips. Then have children read and dramatize the poem.

Apple-Pickin' Time

By Dr. Maggie Allen

I'm going to pick an apple
Right from the tree.
(Reach high overhead)
I'm going to choose a red one,
Round and firm as can be.
(Pick an apple and feel its roundness)
I'm going to take a big bite
And crunch to the core.
(Take a big bite)
I like it so much,
I think I'll pick one more!

Listening Post

Create a medley of songs about fall and tape-record them as the class sings them during circle time. Place the tape in the center, and let children listen to themselves on tape and sing along quietly.

Writing and Illustrating Center

Have children make a five senses rebus book about fall. Ahead of time, create step books, (page 129), and place them in the center with a variety of writing materials, fall stickers, stamps and stamp pads, cutout fall shapes, and stencils. Have children copy the text in the example into their premade books. Ask children to add pictures to finish their poems. For children who are ready, invite them to add words with their pictures.